THE
GARDENERS

Also by Shirley du Boulay
CICELY SAUNDERS:
the Founder of the Modern
Hospice Movement

THE GARDENERS

SHIRLEY DU BOULAY

—— VISITS ——

ROY LANCASTER • GEOFFREY SMITH • FRANCES PERRY

BILL SOWERBUTTS • ALAN TITCHMARSH • SHEILA MACQUEEN

ALAN GEMMELL • PERCY THROWER • MARY SPILLER

JOHN BROOKES • STEFAN BUCZACKI • CLAY JONES

—— IN THEIR OWN GARDENS ——

HODDER AND STOUGHTON

LONDON SYDNEY AUCKLAND TORONTO

British Library Cataloguing in Publication Data
Du Boulay, Shirley
The gardeners
1. Gardeners – Great Britain – Biography
I. Title
635'.092'2 SB61

ISBN 0 340 38112 4

Art Editor: Roger Judd
Design: Osborn & Stephens

Hodder and Stoughton Editorial Office: 47 Bedford Square, London WC1B 3DP

FOR
J.F.X.

CONTENTS

ACKNOWLEDGMENTS

My thanks are due especially to Mary Spiller, who checked the typescript for consistency of nomenclature (though she bears no responsibility for any errors remaining) and to Margaret Body, my editor, whose enthusiasm and encouragement did much to make the writing of this book such a pleasurable experience.

PREFACE

Every Friday evening I, along with over 3,000,000 other amateur gardeners, sit at the feet of the gurus of gardening on *Gardeners' World*; every Sunday afternoon I listen avidly to the advice offered on *Gardeners' Question Time*; I seize any chance to read the gardening columns in whatever newspaper or periodical comes to hand. I learn and I am indebted to this galaxy of gardening stars – for their knowledge and advice, their good humour, their patience, their enthusiasm.

I began to wonder about them. When did they first come to love what John Evelyn calls 'this labour full of tranquillity and satisfaction'? How did they train? What jobs have they held? How, in fact, did they come to be numbered among the horticultural élite, the friends and counsellors of so many amateur gardeners? Above all I wondered what their own gardens were like. Do they practise what they preach? Are their gardens models of textbook excellence, every plant in perpetual perfect health? What do they grow? What is their attitude to their gardens – are they obsessed by them, do they worry about them, do they enjoy them? Are they, in their gardens, very much like the rest of us, or does their professional training set them apart? Do they indeed have gardens at all? Perhaps they would rather do something else with their spare time?

These twelve good gardeners and true allowed me to satisfy my curiosity and write this book. I am grateful for their co-operation, for their hospitality and kindness when I visited them, for their patience with a horticultural amateur, for checking what I wrote with care but without editorial interference, and for lending precious transparencies.

What did I find? I found they have much in common, these twelve gardeners. They all find gardening relaxing; they delight in the freedom to do what they want in their own gardens; they all grow the plants they talk and write about; they none of them feel that their gardens are ever finished, nor do they want to. Their professional skill and confidence prevents them worrying too much; in any case at home they do not garden for other people. If visitors like their gardens, they are pleased, but their private gardens are for them.

But more than their similarities, I found a delightful diversity. Gardeners are a blessed breed, each with his own attitude to his garden, his own priorities, his own special pleasures. To rejoice with me in this endless variety, to explore what makes each gardener unique – please read on.

S du B
Oxfordshire, January 1985

ROY LANCASTER

A LIVING LIBRARY

ONE summer day, over thirty years ago, a keen young naturalist was returning from a bird-watching trip. He was walking past a potato patch on his way back to school, when a plant caught his eye. It was not a potato plant, he knew what a potato plant looked like well enough, but what was it? Something compelled him to climb the fence and pick this solitary stranger. He took it back and looked it up in the picture book in the school library – it was not there. An enterprising master sent it to the local museum at Bolton – they did not know it. It was sent on to the University of Manchester's Botany Department – no one there had ever seen such a plant. They in turn sent the plant, by now presumably slightly bedraggled, to the British Museum which, to the school-boy who had never been further south than Manchester in all his fourteen years, seemed like the other side of the moon. Eventually the letter arrived, it was a Mexican tobacco plant, *Nicotiana rustica*, and it was the first time it had ever been found in Lancashire, only the second time it had ever been found wild in the British Isles. The observant school-boy was Roy Lancaster, now one of Britain's most distinguished plantsmen.

At the time Roy's interest was in birds, but somehow birds kept leading him to plants. Just as his sensational first find in the plant world was made on his way back from watching birds, so he met his first botanical guru through the Bolton Field Naturalists Society, which he had joined in order to study birds. During the winter months there were lectures in a local theatre, on Saturday afternoons in summer and autumn there were bird-watching rambles. But sometimes these rambles were in search of the botanical rather than the ornithological, and this was how Roy met the first of many people who were to influence him – Mr Jackson.

Mr Jackson was a self-taught field naturalist, a rarity even in those days. He was a man who could identify wild flowers without recourse to books; who did not retain botanical Latin but always used the common English names; who was keen on folklore and knew which plants had medicinal or culinary uses; best of all, perhaps, someone who knew stories about the plants. He took Roy under his

Hamamelis vernalis **'Sandra', which originated twenty years ago as a rogue seedling in Hillier's Nursery.**

wing and as they walked along the country lanes he would point out crosswort, celandines, Jack-by-the-hedge, lady's bedstraw, picking samples of each as he named them. Then, towards the end of the afternoon, he would go through the flowers and ask Roy if he could remember the names. At first he couldn't, but he was so touched by the effort Mr Jackson was making for him that he felt the least he could do was try. In any case he wanted to be able to tell other people the stories that so fascinated him.

Soon the names became familiar as he began, plant by plant, experience by experience, to bank the vast wealth of knowledge he was to acquire; his roots as a plantsman are in the English wild flowers and in such early memories as walking through a Pennine woodland into a wet area in a clearing and coming across a host of globe flowers. 'Seeing all those healthy plants with rich glossy leaves and pale yellow orbs scattered throughout the glade – it stopped me in my tracks – I've never forgotten that. I've seen them elsewhere since, I've seen them by the million, but I've never forgotten that first experience.'

Someone else who encouraged him at that time was Charles Edward Shaw, a vicar who came to be known as 'the Weed King of the North'. Vicar Shaw, as Roy always called him, would travel all over the country taking photographs of a particular group of plants, then give an illustrated lecture. Roy was at the stage of thinking there was one kind of thistle, one dock, one willow; discovering there were in Britain alone fifteen different thistles, thirteen docks, forty willows, was to walk into an Aladdin's cave of delights. The first of Vicar Shaw's lectures he attended was called 'The Thistles of Britain'. He knew the familiar spear thistle, but there was the nodding thistle, the tuberous thistle, the milk thistle, the woolly thistle and the melancholy thistle. Whatever was that? He learnt that it was a single-headed, white-stemmed plant, which nods gently and sometimes, in the right light, looks quite ghostly.

Enthusiasts are quickly drawn to each other. Soon the vicar was taking Roy on plant hunting expeditions round Bolton. They would go off in the vicar's old car – Roy can still smell the leather seats and remember seeing the road passing underneath through a hole in the floor – and drive along the country lanes at five miles an hour. All the way they would be scanning the hedgerows and as soon as one of them saw something interesting or unfamiliar they'd shout *stop*, and go and investigate. This way of looking became so much part of Roy's life that even travelling by train his eyes would never leave the embankments. Something he didn't know, a strange shape, an unusual form, a striking colour, would attract his attention as vividly as a red light flashing on and off; he'd make a note and come back as soon as possible to see what it was. If he was in no hurry on a branch line, he would even get off the train at the next station and walk back until he found the plant. Once he was picked up by the police, curious to know what a solitary boy was doing walking along a remote road in Silverdale carrying a mysterious black box – it was full of plants of course.

When Roy and the vicar had exhausted the fields, streamsides and woods of South Lancashire, they started looking for plants on rubbish dumps and tips, finding the dumps by following the rubbish lorries to their destinations. The

Nicotiana rustica, **Roy Lancaster's sensational first find as a fourteen-year-old schoolboy.**

discovery of the tip used by the Crown Wallpaper Company gave a new dimension to their expeditions   foreign plants. The Crown Wallpaper Company used to import rags from the Middle East on which were sticky or hooked seeds of all kinds. These rags were thrown into great vats of acid where the impurities were separated, the rags would dissolve and the seeds and other solids floated to the surface, eventually being dumped on the tip. The acid served to break down the thick seed coats, so the seeds germinated and there, growing on a Lancashire rubbish tip, were scores of oil palms nine inches high, ice plants as big as lettuces, strange clovers, medics, melilots, mustards and exotic cucumbers – all originating in the Middle East and landing up, by means of commerce, in the north of England.

Hypericum lancasteri, **a new species collected by Roy Lancaster in China and the first plant named after him.**

By then Roy had left school and started work. Like countless boys before him, he had wanted to be an engine driver, excited by the power, the smells, the sense of adventure – he'd spent his free time spotting trains as well as wild life. But when the thought of earning his living became harsh reality he dropped the idea in favour of working in the Bolton Natural History Museum. His father had recently died, so he sought advice from the museum's curator, a man who had become something of a father figure, Mr Alfred Hazelwood. Mr Hazelwood dissuaded him from a career in museums, knowing of his love for wild flowers and the open air and pointing out that he would be miserable spending his working life with stuffed birds and the skins of dead animals. Why didn't he go into horticulture? He telephoned a friend who was the foreman of the local Parks Department, and by the following Monday Roy was at work in Moss Bank Park, Bolton.

He was fortunate. Moss Bank Park had its football fields and bowling greens, its pond and its aviary, its predictable Victorian evergreens; but it also had a big limestone rock garden and a walled area, which had been turned into an old English garden. Further, the two men in charge of these gardens were keen gardeners who knew a great deal about their own particular specialities and were determined to pass their knowledge on to their new recruit. They appreciated Roy's familiarity with wild flowers and their English names, but pointed out that if he wanted to get anywhere in horticulture he must also learn the Latin names. So he had to arrive at work early and spend half an hour in one of the two specialist gardens learning a few botanical names every day. He didn't find it came very easily and still remembers wrestling with 'the three A's' – arabis, aubrietia and alyssum. One was white, one was purple, one was yellow, but which was which? He knew they were all members of the same family, the cabbage family, but that only made the situation more confusing. Here, too, he met his first Chinese plant – the Chinese ragwort, a handsome creeping plant that flowers late in the season. It was his job to thin out the huge patch every five or six months, before it took over the whole garden.

Fremontodendron **California Gold', an evergreen shrub which flowers throughout the summer on a south-facing wall.**

There wasn't much time in Roy's life for sport or girls, not yet anyway; he was finding all the excitement and colour he wanted in the plant world. He had explored, often alone, every valley, nook, crook, hillside and pond within a ten mile radius of Bolton Town Hall; he had found plants in waste areas, disused railways, piles of brick rubble, cemeteries, sand dunes and rubbish tips. He had seen plants growing in different conditions and learnt how a species could vary according to where it was growing. Though he didn't appreciate it at the time, he had learnt a great deal of applied botany. However, his only theoretical education was two years studying at night school, so when, after five years at Bolton Parks, he saw an opportunity to train in the Cambridge Botanic Gardens, he took it.

At Cambridge he particularly enjoyed the regular plant identification tests, which were preceded by a conducted walk round the gardens; Roy still feels indebted to John Gilmour, the Director at the time, now long retired. Gilmour would tell the students the name of the plant and what it meant, where it came from in the wild, who first found it and who brought it to this country, the kind of plants with which it might grow in association and little stories and anecdotes about it. He was doing for foreign plants what Mr Jackson had done for British wild plants – providing them with a context. Then as before, Roy was fascinated; he absorbed the information as eagerly as a thirsty camel drinking water.

Roy Lancaster collected seed from this Golden Pomegranate growing in Peking's Forbidden City.

The compulsory botany classes were another matter. Needing the stimulus of the living plant, he simply couldn't retain what he regarded as the dry details of the plant's anatomy, physiology and chemistry. He would find himself doodling, dreaming of far away places where he would one day go in search of plants, thinking, too, of his new-found heroes, the plant hunters Douglas, Wilson, Forrest and Kingdon Ward.

When the time came for Roy to leave the Cambridge Botanic Gardens and look for a job, John Gilmour invited him to stay there, on the staff, but admitted that he would gain more experience by moving on. So he joined Hillier's Nursery near Winchester.

An American once wrote to Roy, complaining that his companions on a plant hunting expedition were only interested in rhododendrons. 'Me,' he wrote, 'I'm interested in anything with chlorophyll.' Roy's sentiments entirely, except that he would add mushrooms and toadstools. So working at Hillier's, where he was allowed, indeed encouraged, to operate on a broad front, suited him so well that he was to stay there for eighteen years.

When he started work, he liked to explain his job by saying, 'I'm a roguer and a sexer.' As a roguer, he would check through saleable plants looking for rogues among almost look-alike varieties of plants – Japanese maples, camellias, dwarf conifers. A sexer, self-evidently, would decide, in plants such as hollies where it was relevant, whether they were male or female.

Early on Roy became involved with cataloguing, for him a new field and one on which he was to make a considerable mark. He had been learning nomenclature, one way or another, since his first trips with Mr Jackson, learning

the English and colloquial names of wild flowers; he had also spent hours teaching himself botanical Latin. His journey to knowledge has much to teach those who are still struggling on the way. When he was at Bolton Parks he obtained basic information from simple plant books, then he made lists; one of colours: *rubra* – red, *viridis* – green; another of words which reveal the plant's origin: *silvatica* – of the woods, *americana* – American, *australis* – no, not Australian, southern, *formosa* – not from the island but the adjective, lovely. No doubt there was a shorter but treasured list – *wilsonii, fortunei, douglasii* . . . As the names acquired meaning, so he found them easier to remember. He would then test his memory on the two miles to and from work, a route which passed many good gardens. He would aim for instant recognition, chanting the names quickly under his breath. '*Campanula carpatica, Rhododendron ponticum, Phlomis fruticosa* . . .'

Hillier's is famous mainly for its trees and shrubs, but they also grow herbaceous plants, alpines, grasses and ferns, and it was on these non-woody subjects that Roy first came to be regarded as an expert. Writing descriptions of the plants meant being where he wanted to be – with the plants themselves; and the names of plants had always stirred his imagination. 'A plant's name is a key to its history. Without that key you might get to the door, but not through it. The name is not important for its own sake, but for what it does; it unlocks a door to wonderful stories, history, adventure, romance even.'

His arrival at Hillier's in 1962 coincided with early preparations for their centenary, which they were marking with a *Centenary Catalogue of Trees and Shrubs*, and he was soon closely involved with it. When that was completed, the idea was mooted that the catalogue should be revised and extended and Roy was asked to look after it. The more he pondered, the more he felt that here was an opportunity to do something worthwhile, something lasting. Hillier's were the largest growers of hardy woody plants in the world, selling the greatest variety. Surely there was room for a publication that reflected their position in horticulture, something with really good descriptions that would help the student as well as the keen amateur, something more than just a nursery catalogue? Gradually Roy's idea began to catch on. The descriptions became longer, the accompanying information more detailed. Harold Hillier himself started contributing little anecdotes from his unrivalled experience and knowledge, for instance how he collected his original stock of a wild honeysuckle, *Lonicera implexa,* while on his honeymoon in Gibraltar in 1934.

When Hillier's *Manual of Trees and Shrubs* was eventually published, after five years of writing, editing, correcting, rewriting, (the printers wanted to keep the galley proofs to offer to the Printer's Museum, they had never seen anything like it) it was a handsome volume of nearly 600 pages containing lively, informative descriptions of 7,000 plants. It was a break through, very soon it was a bestseller – no catalogue had ever sold so well. You have to look quite hard to find Roy's name in the introduction, but no one denies his role in its creation.

Roy gained experience of most things at Hillier's – most things, that is, except business – Harold Hillier had never looked on him as someone who would excel

Diplacus glutinosus **hybrid; a Californian woody-stemmed version of our common monkey musk, thriving on a south-facing wall.**

Deutzia calycosa, **a hardy summer-flowering shrub, new to western gardens. It was collected in 1981 from the Cangshan mountains in south-west China.**

on the business side. He not only wrote catalogues, he worked in the drawing office, designing landscapes and planting plans, he helped plan and stage exhibitions, he advised customers, both in the nursery and in their own gardens and collections. In 1965 Harold Hillier decided he needed a horticultural botanist to work permanently in the Arboretum, checking the plants in his collection, making sure they were correctly named, labelled and recorded. For some years Roy supervised this, in 1970 being officially made the first curator of the Arboretum.

One of his jobs as curator, one which he most enjoyed and still misses, was taking groups round the Arboretum. They might be learned groups from the International Dendrology Society, specialist tours looking at conifers, an individual writing a thesis on magnolias. They could be students from horticultural colleges, keen amateurs, blind people or children – handicapped children, deprived children, children from urban areas who hadn't seen many trees, let alone an arboretum.

He would watch the group assemble, assessing what they were likely to enjoy, then, with the imagination of the natural teacher, involve every member of the group in his own passion for trees. If they were a young group, he would take them not so much on a walk as on an adventure, jumping across streams, creeping through bamboo thickets, climbing hills; he'd make them laugh, set competitions, throw in the odd brush with education – pointing out a gum tree from Australia, a fir from the Himalayas. Always he encouraged contact. 'Feel the bark, feel it, don't just stand and look at it. A tree is a living thing, you need to be part of it. Climb it, put your arms round it, lean against it. Feel that hard bark, that peeling bark, feel the ridges, listen to the leaves crackling underfoot.' Blind people he didn't need to encourage – they established contact immediately, but so that he could enter more fully into their experience, he would sometimes walk around the Arboretum with his eyes closed or go out at night, feeling the trees as a blind person might, listening to them. Roy had found yet another talent, his latent gifts of communication had found expression.

He was also beginning to fulfil the dreams that had sustained him as he doodled his way through the botany classes at Cambridge – he began to travel. In 1971 he went to East Nepal for three months on his first expedition, bringing back seeds and plants; the next year he was sent to Iran. The Shah of Persia wanted a Botanic Garden, Hillier's were supplying some of the plants and it was Roy who supervised the loading of two great trucks, then flew to Teheran to greet them and spend a month on the site. Before leaving for home he spent 'two marvellous days in paradise' – paradise in this case being the Caspian Forest in the Elburz Mountains, where some of the plants he had chosen for the Shah originated. He saw the begonia-leaved lime, *Tilia begoniifolia*; the woolly-twigged spindle, *Euonymus velutinus*; the Persian ironwood, *Parrotia persica*, named after a German naturalist Herr Parrot, who climbed Mount Ararat in 1934 and was the first man to do so – or the second if you count Noah. Roy must have had to pinch himself to make sure it was really happening.

The cost of running a large arboretum is formidable. By 1978 Hillier's had to come to terms with the harsh truth, they could no longer afford to finance it, it simply wasn't bringing enough money into the nursery coffers. So Harold Hillier made a gift of his arboretum to the Hampshire County Council. Roy didn't see himself as a local government officer and his impulse was to leave immediately, but he was persuaded to stay to ensure a smooth hand-over. He stayed just two years, the change of management was accomplished. He decided to leave and go freelance.

He envisaged a life of writing, lecturing and advisory work – perhaps he could also do some television? To begin with business was slow and irregular, but he persisted, tackling the situation with northern directness. Gradually the work began to come in. He had been twice to China on botanical expeditions when Granada Television asked him to do a piece for a magazine programme called *Down to Earth*, showing the local boy who had travelled the world back in Bolton, where it had all begun. Then there was *In Search of the Wild Asparagus*, a series on wild flowers, in which he revisited the places he used to explore with Mr Jackson and Vicar Shaw. *Gardeners' World* invited him to take part on their regular programmes as well as a special series, *Shades*.

Here was a new sort of television gardener, so predictably there were, at first, a few critics. Did people really want to know that such and such a plant is one of 560 saxifrages and that it grows on a rock ledge in the middle of China? Would they not prefer to learn how to grow lettuce and prune roses? It soon became clear from the enthusiastic audience reaction that there was plenty of room for both. Roy had found his own corner in the television world, where he could do what he loved to do, tell stories, talk about the history of plants and add a new dimension to gardening for millions of delighted viewers.

Roy's own garden is a living extension to his library, somewhere he can gain personal experience of the plants he writes and talks about, a home for the seeds, plants and cuttings he is given and brings back from the plant hunting expeditions which are now such an important part of his life. And just as a library is first a place to keep books and only secondly a place to make beautiful, so Roy's first need is to accommodate plants. He would like to think in terms of vistas and colour schemes, but to do that effectively involves a more generous attitude to space than he can afford, for instance by massing plants in groups. As every plant duplicated means one less new plant, the lure of landscape design has had to be resisted. The garden is also a place for his wife and children and, considering the family's combined needs, it is small, only a quarter of an acre.

Making the best use of his limited space is a problem Roy approaches with a bold simplicity. An area of lawn has been allocated especially to the children, where they can feel free to play games, scuff the grass and tumble through the climbing frame. (There are not any no-go areas, Roy simply encourages them to treat his plants gently, as they would a kitten or a chick.) The rest of the garden, both the small front garden and the larger, south-facing piece of land at the back, is for plants. The main part of his garden is divided into four equal compartments. One is a Chinese garden, in the sense that everything in it is something he has collected in China; two others he uses for a mixed bag of plants he is given, plants he buys, plants that remind him of people, events, places – like the ornamental onions bringing back memories of his days at Bolton Parks; the fourth section is for vegetables and for growing on plants he has started as seeds and cuttings. An imaginative space-saving idea is that where he wants a protective hedge he uses, not the familiar hedging plants we are all urged to buy, but a selection of some of his special shrubs. These informal lines dividing the various parts of the garden allow him to accommodate more plants while giving him unique hedges.

Though they have only lived there for two years, already the garden contains what must be one of the most extraordinary collections of plants in any private garden, each one with a story, a history.

Some are especially interesting because they originated as rogue seedlings – like the *Hamamelis vernalis* 'Sandra'. Twenty years ago a propagator called Peter Dummer was looking through 2,000 seedlings of *Hamamelis vernalis*, when he came across one that had plum purple tips instead of the green he was expecting. He planted it up and watched it. In the autumn, when all the other *vernalis* turned

Rosa omeiensis **is widespread in Hubei and Sichuan provinces in China. Its name refers to Mount Omei, one of China's four most sacred mountains.**

butter yellow, this one ignited into orange, scarlet and red; he called it 'Sandra' after his daughter. Another unpublicised plant *Stachyurus chinensis* 'Magpie' remained for years as a single shrub, growing by the old gaol wall in Hillier's Winchester Nurseries. When the *Manual* was being written they decided that it should be propagated and named, so they called it 'Magpie' to suggest the striking variegated leaves.

Many of Roy's plants remind him of old friends, like *Drimys winteri*, a handsome evergreen shrub from South America given to him by a friend, the late Basil Fox, who was Curator of the University of Aberystwyth Botanic Gardens, or a very beautiful cherry, one of Roy's favourites, 'Kursar', which was raised by the late Captain Collingwood Ingram, the leading western authority on Japanese cherries.

One of the best roses for a large garden, *Rosa roxburghii*. Viciously armed with fat green prickly hips, it is also known as the 'Burr rose' or the 'Chestnut rose'.

There is one area of the Lancasters' garden which provides conditions as near Mediterranean as anything in England outside a hot house. It is the south-facing back of the house, exposed to full sun as the previous owner had cut down all the trees. Roy uses this hot, dry wall as a protective host for some of his treasures. There is a buddleia, *B. alata*, a powerful shrub already fifteen feet high and only recently identified by a Dutch expert. This was grown from seed collected in the Cangshan, a mountain range in south-west China, when Roy was there in May 1981, one of five British members of a Sino–British expedition. All the seeds and plants went back to the Edinburgh Botanic Gardens and were then distributed amongst the members of the expedition and the subscribers. It is too soon yet for many to have flowered, but all are growing well and Roy expects that most will be flowering quite soon. The wall also supports an Australian mimosa, already eighteen feet high, which he hopes will soon reach the eaves of the house, its delicate leaves blending happily with the grey foliage of the evergreen *Ozothamnus rosmarinifolius* 'Silver Jubilee'.

Pride of place must surely go to a pomegranate, collected by Roy from the Forbidden City in Peking. He saw them in tubs, all bearing rosy red fruits save one, whose fruits were a golden yellow. He had never heard of a golden pomegranate and has still found no reference to it, but the *pomme d'or* of mediaeval legend floated into his mind. Could this be the golden fruited pomegranate, the unique possession of the Emperor, the only one in his kingdom? Roy was handling the fruit as the fantasy unfurled and his thumb nail somehow slipped under the skin. He hastily wiped the seeds on to his handkerchief before an official came up to admonish him. He hopes that this plant from the Forbidden City will reward him with golden fruit; he will have to stay his curiosity for at least another five years, but it will be worth the wait.

On the other side of the patio, opposite the exotic plants which are covering the south wall and edging the children's lawn, is a hollow wall filled with smaller sun-loving plants – *Salvia castanea, Convolvulus cneorum, Ceanothus gloriosus* and several varieties of *Cistus*. Most delicate, most charming, is the *Dierama pulcherrimum*, sometimes called angel's fishing rod, a native of South Africa and thriving in this favoured position.

Roy has no hierarchy of plants, his love for them, remember, embraces

Lobelia laxiflora, another plant which enjoys Roy Lancaster's south-facing wall.

'anything with chlorophyll'. He would not, however, deny the special place occupied by anything from China. He has been to China several times, often as the leader of a botanical group. He has seen acers, cornus and sorbus in their wild state in the Chinese Alps; philadelphus, deutzias, roses, buddleias, rhododendrons on the Tibetan border; exotic aquatics, even the sacred lotus, in the Summer Palace in Peking; he has seen the golden poppywort, *Meconopsis integrifolia*, within yards of the spot in the Zheduo Pass above Kangding where Ernest Wilson first found it in 1903. His first contact with wild Chinese plants was such an emotional moment he could barely see them for the tears that overcame him. Small wonder, then, that he grows Chinese plants, not just in the favoured position on the patio, but all over his garden. He has Chinese ferns from Hangzhou, of which it is said 'In heaven there is Paradise, on earth there is Hangzhou' – a remark no less charming for being attributed to at least seven other places. There's a *Viburnum chingii* grown from seed collected in south-west China and one of only two specimens in the country; the Chinese dove tree, *Davidia involucrata*; and an *Epimedium acuminatum* which not only has huge purple and white flowers and the longest flowering period of any epimedium, but which hides a secret in its leaves – the underneath is a glaucous blue. Roy collected the seedlings from Mount Omei, one of the four mountains most sacred to Buddhists in China. He believes they have not previously been introduced to western cultivation.

One of the plants of which he is proudest is a hypericum, the first plant to be named after him and ensure that his name joins his heroes in the plant catalogues. Dr Norman Robson, a friend who specialises in them, complained that all his shrubby hypericums from China were old specimens from the early decades of the century or before – he would love to have some fresh material. This request fired Roy with an enthusiasm for the genus which amused the Chinese members of the expedition so much that they couldn't pass a plant without saying, 'Here hypericum – new species, new species.' Dr Robson was so overwhelmed by the plants that Roy collected him – they included at least four new species and still more new varieties – that this one, from the western hills of Kunming, now bears the name *Hypericum lancasteri*.

Significantly Roy calls the large greenhouse at the bottom of his garden the powerhouse. Here his seeds and cuttings spend their early lives, it is his research laboratory, the place where the introduction of new species and varieties begins to become a reality. Plantsmen are generous with their plants, liking to share and to give. Seed from foreign parts is always distributed widely to increase the plants' chance of survival. 'The whole point about garden plant conservation,' says Roy, 'is that if you want to save a plant, then give it away.' This statement, with its almost Biblical ring, sums up the generosity of the plant hunting fraternity, a generosity not unmixed with a healthy rivalry as to whose seed will germinate first, produce the largest plants, flower earliest. Those who are to receive the seed are, of course, carefully chosen. Roy will give plants or seeds away for many reasons – from sheer generosity to the knowledge that the plant may get too big for his own garden, but he will only give them to people who will care for them. The plantsman's plants are his children and must go to good homes.

Roy doesn't normally grow anything that requires heat, though he does have an electrical heater set at just above freezing to ensure his greenhouse is frost free. Sometimes, however, he is spurred on to ambitions which at first seemed unrealistic, as when he saw pictures of two Mongolian plants, *Hedysarum scoparium*, a lax, slender-stemmed shrub with racemes of purple pea-flowers, and *Limonium aureum*, a golden form of sea lavender. They were amongst the loveliest things he had seen in a long time, but what was the point of growing desert plants in Great Britain? By one of those strokes of fortune, a week later he received seeds of those very same plants from a friend in Shanghai. How could he spurn them? He shared out the seeds and sowed some himself. If in years to come these plants come into general cultivation in this country, it will be thanks to an exchange between Shanghai and England and Roy's impulsive response.

It is fitting to end with the small patch of lawn in front of the Lancasters' house. It had been made by some previous owner with turf from a local meadow, and when the Lancasters arrived Roy found over forty different species of English wild plants. He did not go into action with the weedkillers to produce a perfect grass lawn, but treated it as downland turf. He is rewarded by autumn lady's tresses, pink centaury and a host of small plants that remind him of his childhood rambles and those happy days with Mr Jackson and the Weed King of the North. He has seen plants in their natural habitats all over the world, written about them, talked about them, marvelled at them, but the English wild flowers, where it all started, will never lose their special place in his affections.

GEOFFREY SMITH

A GOURMET FEAST

OUTSIDE Geoffrey Smith's sitting room is a garden seat, inscribed with the legend 'Be still – listen'. It says much about him. Professionally trained gardener though he is, versed also in such writers on the countryside as Richard Jefferies, Edward Thomas, Gilbert White, Cobbett, Williamson and Hudson, at heart he feels he is a peasant, with a peasant's pleasure in simply growing plants. He loves to be quiet, to stand and look. His favourite companion on a garden visit is Roy Lancaster, who can stand silently before a plant as long as he. Their shared passion once led them to burst out laughing, as they suddenly realised that they had lingered so long they were striking matches to see rhododendron leaves; their subsequent conversation was still in full flood at two o'clock in the morning. Anyone who questions the sincerity of Geoffrey Smith's enthusiasm can be reassured – he is a gardener, first, last and all the way through.

Peasant-like, too, he needs to be master of his own fate; living by the rule book is not something he can tolerate. As a young apprentice studying for a diploma with the Forestry Commission he distrusted and disliked the bureaucracy he found there, and his keen questioning of the official pamphlets worried the foreman, leading to his resignation after only four months. He found his next job, growing commercial crops, bored him, though in this case he was the manager, and he left. Even as a student at Askham Bryan, the Yorkshire College of Horticulture, where he was happy and successful, ending up as head student, he was in trouble over rules and regulations. So keen was he on his studies that he would creep down in the middle of the night to use the magnificent library and microscopes, somehow surviving on four hours' sleep; on one occasion he exasperated the lecturers by spotting a contradiction in the current tuition on the structure of clay and forcing them to admit that, at that time, there was in fact no

Geoffrey Smith's garden on the North Yorkshire Moors. 'Gardening on a hillside is a compromise between what you would like to grow and what the wind will let you grow.

answer. He is still grateful to his father, whose realistic respect for paper qualifications led to his going to Askham Bryan and learning the theory behind what he had been doing. Up till then he had little idea of why he was doing what he did. He put nitrate on cabbages, mulched rhododendrons with peat, planted some lilies four inches deep, some six, simply because he was told to; he had little knowledge of nomenclature, the chemistry of soils, plant pathology or entomology. The two-year course, which he managed to do in one year, taught him that even though it was the practical application of gardening that appealed to him, there was a real value in combining theory and practice. After leaving college he took a job at Rosewarne, a government research station in Cornwall, but that didn't suit him either; he found no room for initiative, improvisation or practising economy, but he did enjoy the cricket and just lasted for the duration of the season.

So he wrote to Harlow Car asking for a job. He was offered a place as a journeyman gardener, a demotion, taking him back to the level he was at before he went to college, nevertheless he accepted. After three weeks he was made one of two foremen and after three months he was asked to be superintendent. So at last, at twenty-six, he found both independence and a challenge which was to sustain him for twenty years.

Rhododendron Lady Chamberlain '**Exbury**'. **Geoffrey Smith considers this one of the aristocrats of the genus.**

Harlow Car is the Northern Horticultural Society's garden – it is to the north as Wisley and Kew are to the south. There he had, for most of the time, eight people working under him, sixty-eight acres of largely undeveloped fields and no resources apart from voluntary subscriptions. At the outset the director said to him, 'If you make mistakes you are responsible. If you do well, we take the credit.' He knew just where he was and it suited him. He loved every minute. Initiative and imagination spurred them on, as he and his helpers pulled six-ton stones off the moors five miles away to build the rock garden. Somehow they lifted the huge weights with a block and tackle, brought them back on a trailer and man-handled them into position. Everything was done by hand on a shoe-string budget. There was no special equipment, only a tractor and a trailer which they had been given. Here was scope for ingenuity, still more for creativity. If Harlow Car is now one of the glories of the north, some of the credit must be Geoffrey Smith's.

Harlow Car provided a tied house, so it wasn't until 1974, when he left to concentrate on writing and broadcasting, that the Smiths had their own house and, at last, their own garden. House hunting proved very difficult. Most of the houses they liked were too expensive and Geoffrey, not surprisingly, insisted on

The brilliantly coloured *Primula rosea*, which enjoys a shady corner. It is the first primula to flower in the garden.

Geoffrey Smith's favourite *Meconopsis. M. Grandis* 'Slieve Donard'. It was bred by the late Leslie Slinger, of the famous Slieve Donard nursery.

The autumn gentian *Gentiana sino-ornata*. 'No garden with an acid soil should be without it'.

living in the country. 'A hen house on the Yorkshire Moors, a boat on the Ouse, a caravan and come home for meals – anything rather than live in the town.' He must have infuriated his family. When they found their present house, part of which was condemned, he never looked at the house, never noticed the damp, just gazed out of the window at the half acre that was to be his own, planning his garden. For the first time in his life he could do just what he wanted, after half a lifetime spent gardening for other people, doing what they wanted.

The half acre over which he was dreaming was a patch of rough grass, 800 feet above sea level, looking south over the North Yorkshire Moors. All that was planted was a conifer hedge, which he eventually had to pull down, as the snow flattened the branches. The soil is Grade Four Moorland, just on the acid side of neutral, very poor and light. Inevitably he suffers from the gardening hazard predictable in the north. 'If you walk outside with a cup of tea when the wind is blowing, it blows the milk straight out and leaves you with the plain tea.' Yorkshire wit apart, it is very windy.

Now, ten years later, it is immaculate and sparkling; the garden of a professional gardener who loves plants and knows how to grow them. He dislikes large masses of colour, preferring to place his plants in intimate groups, one enhancing the other. Early in March a witch hazel or variegated holly grows out of a carpet of snowdrops, the wine red *Daphne mezereum* is surrounded by light purple crocuses, yellow crocuses grow at the feet of a golden *Thuja occidentalis* 'Rheingold'. Each grouping leads the eye on to another; each season has its own focal points of colour, habit or texture.

The permanent features – rockery, shade border, pool, table beds, hollow wall, herb garden, choice border, greenhouse, cold frame and pool – surround the house in a pleasing and friendly way, enclosed by a low stone wall and blended together both by a skilful design which grew organically (he does not plan on paper or attempt to do everything at once) and by his refusal to confine any plant to one area of the garden. So alpines grow not only in the rockery, but in the hollow walls and table beds; rhododendrons flourish in the colourful shade border as in the 'choice' border. (He is amazed that people complain about having areas of their garden in shade, as there are so many plants that will not grow anywhere else.) Evergreens provide shelter, form and year round colour. At the moment he does not grow vegetables, but he is planning to put that right soon.

Gardening for Geoffrey Smith is a continual creative process; he moves his plants, apart from a few that are too large or too tender, as freely as most people move their furniture. If he does not like a corner, he adds, alters, removes, until he does. Sometimes he buys plants on impulse, not sure where they will go, sometimes he chooses carefully and systematically – recently he acquired a collection of dog tooth violets. Sometimes he is given treasured plants by gardening friends and colleagues. But mostly he grows from seed and cuttings, delighting in every sort of propagation. He is particularly pleased by a group of *Iris danfordiae*, which usually need planting every year as they split up into little bulblets that are not big enough to flower; he fed them so heavily that they

responded by flowering again the next year. The frequent presence of television
cameras often involves changes more radical than even he might wish, but he is
not a whit disturbed. Recently a favourite border had to be almost completely
dug up; his reaction was simply that now he would reinstate it, making it even
more choice. His garden is as he wishes it to be, furnished, but never completely
finished.

The over-all effect delights and intrigues. So come closer and see what
Geoffrey Smith has packed into one of his 'choice corners'. In a relatively small
garden (he would like to have at least four acres) he tries to avoid shrubs like
forsythia, with its short spell of glory, choosing less usual plants that are more
subtle, give more value throughout the year. In one small bed, quite near the
house, he has *Rosa rubrifolia, Berberis thunbergii* 'Fire King' and *Erica carnea*
'Myreton Ruby', their dark reds setting off a deutzia with double white flowers,
D. scabra 'Candidissima', and a philadelphus he has only recently met, 'Silver
Cascade'. *Cyclamen coum* gives winter colour and the hardy geranium, *G.
subcaulescens* 'Splendens', which he uses all over the garden, flowers throughout
the summer. Among these he has planted *Alstroemeria ligtu* hybrids and lilies, *L.
monadelphum* and *L. regale*. He is pleased with this combination, so perhaps he
will not find it necessary to alter it for a year or two.

Embothrium coccineum, the Chilean fire bush. Geoffrey Smith waited ten years for it to flower and feels it should be more widely grown.

But he may, for he is endearingly contradictory. He knows, as indeed any amateur knows, that the sensible gardener grows along with his soil, situation and climate. He admits that if he gardened on lime, obviously he wouldn't attempt rhododendrons, much though he loves them. But, within reason, he cannot resist trying anything he fancies, nor can he resist a challenge. Sometimes plants have astonished him by surviving, and he has learnt that a plant will stand one degree of adversity, for instance a badly drained soil, as long as it doesn't have to put up with an adverse climate as well. He is rightly proud of his ability to grow plants successfully, so he is sad, even mildly humiliated, that he cannot persuade hardy orchids to grow under his conditions. He does not hide behind the unsuitable climate and soil, but says plaintively, 'I should be able to persuade them into doing a little better than they do.' He has also had to admit defeat and remove a *Sorbus mitchellii*, which just couldn't make a strong enough root to support itself on such a windy site. Nor will he give up his ambition to grow fruit: inspired by seeing the luxuriant groves round Evesham, he refuses to be discouraged. A more realistic ambition is to make a wild garden, to see primroses growing in a hazel copse through a carpet of emerald green moss, or snowdrops in bloom round a silver-leaved holly on a cold day in early February.

While he was filming his television series *The World of Flowers*, he had the good fortune to see many flowers growing in their natural state. *Narcissus triandrus* arching across a hillside in Spain, *Gentiana verna* carpeting Teesdale, *Primula marginata* in the Maritime Alps. Seeing them in the wild, so abundant, blending so harmoniously with their surroundings, he announced, 'No way would I bring them into my garden. I hated zoos as a kiddie, I didn't want to see animals in cages and I don't want to see flowers in the wrong place.' But in practice? He grows them of course. Or at least some of them. He is happy to have *Narcissus asturiensis* in his borders, but not *N. triandrus*; he delights in *Primula farinosa* but not cowslips, plants that belong to the open meadows. He gives no reason for this inconsistency. Why, indeed, should he?

Pruning, which some find painful, some irresistible, likewise reveals this contradictory pull. He ponders over a weeping pear. Should he take the top off and encourage it to grow into a mound? As he pauses, one shares his anguish at taking the secateurs to it, his vision of the dense shrub it could become. Then 'Ah, let it grow.'

The garish dazzle of 'Paint Box' primroses in the miniature rock garden in the centre of the lawn does not, however, reveal any inconsistency. He loves the true wild primrose to distraction and finds these modern developments vulgar. 'I give them to my brother, he likes the gor-blimey.' However he spares them a little garden room, as he feels he cannot talk or write about anything with authority unless he has studied them at close quarters. Sometimes it works to his advantage. Last spring he sowed a packet of the new John Innes hybrid anemones, strictly in the course of duty, and was rewarded by weeks of colour in the subtle shades that he prefers.

In fact there is very little that Geoffrey Smith does not enjoy growing and does not grow with conspicuous success. His wide interest and knowledge dates from when he was the youngest of five men working in a private garden where his father was head gardener – which meant, incidentally, that he got stricter, not preferential, treatment. It was a small enough garden for all five to do everything, there was not the specialisation inevitable in a large estate. There he raised pot plants for indoor decoration, worked with vegetables, fruit, shrubs, roses, herbaceous plants and alpines; he tended the sweeping lawns and looked after a woodland garden, a riot of anemones, daffodils, scillas and snowdrops. In short he was a good, all-round practical gardener before he went to college and learnt the theory.

This early training established the broad spectrum of plants whose tastes and inclinations he understands. Today, though he may upset lovers of *Garrya elliptica* by dismissing it as depressing and funereal, that unfortunate shrub is alone in receiving his condemnation. He grows trilliums and rhododendrons, cassiopes and hebes, pelargoniums and fuchsias, hellebores and water lilies, vegetables and herbs, alpines and, of course, trees – 'the ultimate in gardening,

Lilies growing on the terrace. This is a new variety bred by Edward Macrae in North America, *Lilium* 'Campfire'.

Geoffrey Smith grows many different sorts of geraniums, but if he had to restrict himself to one, it would be this – *Geranium cinereum* 'Ballerina', hard to beat for all round durability.

your toe–hold in immortality'. If he had to limit himself, he would choose 'plants with personality', no worse a criterion for being a highly subjective judgement. For him, the 'big five' are lilies, rhododendrons, meconopsis, gentians and primulas.

He sees gardening as an ever-expanding vista and is still keen to know more and more about more and more, rather than to specialise, which he sees as stultifying the mind. In any case, 'You could spend your whole life on rhododendrons and still not fully understand them.' This wide vision, together with his delight in sharing his pleasure in plants, combine to make him one of the most popular gardeners on radio and television. He recognises that while ambition can motivate, it can also destroy the things it motivates, but is not ashamed to admit to pleasure in his success. He also finds broadcasting is a stimulus to learn more.

It all started while he was at Harlow Car. He was high up in an oak tree, lopping the top branches, when he saw someone wandering round the garden looking rather lost. Thinking he might need help, he slid down the rope, landing at the feet of the astonished visitor. Over a cup of tea, Geoffrey discovered that he was

Mixed hardy shrubs providing a shelter from the wind. Geoffrey Smith finds this more interesting than the hard line of a formal hedge.

Paul Morby, the producer of the television programme, *Gardening Club*. The meeting led to his first television appearance, an occasion which turned out to be a baptism with fire. He was asked to talk for eighteen minutes on Michaelmas daisies, alone and live – there was little pre-recording in those days. It was to be the first of many. *Direct Lines*, a live programme from Leeds in which listeners ring in with questions and Geoffrey 'stands there like a banana hoping I'll know the answer', *Gardening Club, Dig This, Down the Garden Path,* the weekly radio programme *Gardeners' Question Time, Gardeners' World.* He gardens almost as much on the air as in the earth.

Despite a need to withdraw from the public eye, Geoffrey has a gregarious streak. He enjoys the companionship that making television programmes brings and the situations in which he has found himself. While taking part in *Food for Thought* he suffered from indigestion as a result of tasting fish with new potatoes and cream three times during rehearsals. Once he found himself on the wrong side of a fence while filming on the Yorkshire Moors – with a bull for company. There was one occasion when he took part in a subterfuge that it's hard not to call cheating. They were filming a programme on growing vegetables, recording six programmes in four weeks, from sowing to harvesting. Clearly nature was not going to obey such a schedule, but Geoffrey did not want to let down his producer. He was living in Norfolk at the time, so, taking advantage of its earlier season, he dug up leeks, onions, beetroot and celery, drove to Yorkshire and replanted them. As the cameras rolled, he produced them triumphantly from their new home. 'It's the only time I've cheated – and it wasn't really cheating, just transferring from one garden to another.'

If television forces unnatural speed on its contributors, gardening itself fosters patience. Calm though he appears, Geoffrey Smith says he can be 'madder than a scalded cat' if he feels he has done something badly, if for instance one of his lectures has not gone well. The garden helps him to see the problem in perspective. He takes especial delight in plants that take time to reach maturity – a nectarine or a peach planted as a stone; a fig or grape from cuttings. When he first started work on the garden he planted several crab tree pips, now climbing to fifteen feet and higher. Rarer and even more thrilling, 1984 saw the first flowering of his Chilean fire bush, *Embothrium coccineum*; he had waited a decade for this moment. He finds gardening gives him an appreciation not only of time, but of history, realising that it is not static, but a living, developing link between generation and generation. He likes to remember that the Aztecs were growing dahlias in Mexico when Quetzalcoatl was worshipped, long before Cortes saw them, long before Dr Dahl gave them his name, long before John Fraser brought them to England. He loves to consider how, over the years, they have changed and developed.

Geoffrey Smith considers himself something of a dilettante. 'It's like having a great gourmet feast spread in front of you. You could, if you felt like it, fill yourself absolutely full with the hors d'oeuvre. But if there were a great spread of fifteen courses, I would rather have a little snippet of each and finish off with coffee and biscuits and peppermints. Gardening's like that.'

Geoffrey Smith's garden is now an essential part of his life. He relishes it in all its moods as a wine connoisseur relishes fine burgundies. He is able, unlike many gardeners, to obey the injunction on his garden seat. 'Do you know the nicest time to sit in a garden? It's when you've had a good grafting day in it. And you go out in the quiet of a summer evening and you think. That's the best reason I can think of for gardening. Because it looks nice when you've finished.'

Poolside planting at its peak.

FRANCES PERRY

A PLANTSWOMAN'S GARDEN

WHEN Frances Perry sits at her desk she is surrounded on two sides by her treasured collection of gardening books; the other two look over her garden. She is never far from her garden, seldom out of sight of it. For her, work and leisure, house and garden, are harmoniously united. Her garden is closely planted in three layers, with early bulbs followed by herbaceous perennials, then autumn bulbs and late-flowering shrubs, so her view is never without interest. In summer the house is festooned with hanging containers, and tubs stand on any patch of terrace that has the effrontery to be naked; indoors there are cut flowers and house plants. Frances Perry without plants would be like plants without water.

So it is with people. Since her teens she has been surrounded by gardeners, not through accident of birth, but led to them by early, instinctive choice. Her mother claimed that her interest began at eighteen months, when she fell, head-first, into a tub of liquid manure. Frances herself, perhaps preferring to forget the experience, feels it all started when she was thirteen. Her mother had been given tickets for the Chelsea Flower Show and Frances, despite getting into terrible trouble at school 'for making such a frivolous excuse to take a day off', somehow got permission to go. She was entranced, not only by the women in their over-decorated hats and the gentlemen in their grey toppers (it was in 1921 when such events demanded dress) but by the flowers. There was no hesitation. She knew that this was what she must do. Something, anything, to do with flowers.

She was fortunate in living near Myddelton House, whose garden had been made famous by that great and lovable gardener E. A. Bowles. She had known him all her life and often asked his help in naming her wild flowers, so her mother, who never knew one flower from another and found the whole idea of

Early summer border with delphiniums and peonies.

An effective spring combination of *Magnolia stellata* underplanted with double daffodils.

her daughter being a gardener very odd (why couldn't she be a teacher or work in a bank like anyone else?), sought his advice. He said she should be trained and suggested she went to Swanley Horticultural College, bombed during the 1939–45 war and now part of Wye College. The college decreed that after the two-year theoretical training students should have a year's practical experience in a nursery or large garden. So Frances wrote to three local nurseries, Carter Page, which no longer exists, Stuart Lowe, who still has a pot plant business near Enfield, and Amos Perry. It was Amos Perry, a friend of Bowles, who offered her a place, so her first paid job was at Perry's Hardy Plant Farm.

The Perrys had been nursery gardeners for four generations, Amos being the fifth. When Frances arrived he was adding water gardening and aquatic plants to his business, though there was at the time little interest in the subject. Indeed he used to lament that people laughed at him for growing water plants in tubs. He asked Frances to look after this new venture. 'I used to go off to work as happy as a bird. It was the biggest water-plant nursery in the world at that time and I became so houseproud of these great big glass-houses full of water plants. I wouldn't let anybody come in if they had dirty feet.'

She learnt so quickly that soon Amos Perry, who had been invited to write an article on aquatic plants for *Country Life*, asked her to do it. She was horrified. How did she start? She had never done anything like it before. She locked herself up in an attic where she was so uncomfortable she had nothing to do but write, found she was well able to do it and received fifteen shillings. That led to a book on water gardening which both filled a gap in horticultural literature and established her as an expert in the field.

Those great gardeners, E. A. Bowles and Amos Perry, exercised a strong influence on Frances. Bowles was known to have no time for girls, in any case professional women gardeners in those days were as rare as badgers in daylight, but he always allowed her the run of his large library and told her about his plant treasures, treasures that gardeners the world over came to see. She became very close to him, at one stage visiting Myddelton almost every day, helping him type the notes for his book on anemones, being his 'eyes' when his sight began to fail. Amos Perry's tastes, vigorous and independent, also affected her. He refused to grow any roses except species roses and she still remembers him saying, when she was given a bunch of roses at Chelsea, 'I'm not being seen with you carrying those.' He was a great plantsman, knowing his plants so intimately, remembering them so well, that he could tell her just where, for instance, a *Lesquerella englemanii* grew in 1908. He loved hardy plants, ferns, bulbs, everything hardy, saying, 'If it can't look after itself in winter, it's not worth growing.'

The Perry influence took a more personal turn in 1930, when Frances married Gerald, the eldest son and the sixth generation of gardeners. To him she owes her love of herbaceous plants and the extra dimension he added to her love of propagation. So skilled was he at propagating that he could persuade the most surprising bits of plants to multiply, even day lilies from stem cuttings, something Frances has never known anyone else able to do.

By the time war broke out in 1939 Frances was established as a professional gardener. War had brought its inevitable dearth of trained people and in 1942 Frances was approached by the Middlesex County Council to help with the schools, allotment societies and even army sites, teaching, demonstrating and lecturing. She had only been three weeks in her new post when her chief told her she was to appear on a *Brains Trust* chaired by Freddie Grisewood. As with her first piece of writing, she was terrified. 'I've never forgotten it. There were 2000 people in the marquee, it was war-time and everyone was worried about food. I thought "I've *got* to answer the first question." It was on blackcurrants, which worried me because it was a long time since I'd studied vegetables and soft fruit, but it was all right.'

Her Perry name at first held back her broadcasting career in a BBC which abhorred the faintest whiff of trade advertising. But she was recommended by the Secretary of the Royal Horticultural Society and eventually appeared on a spelling bee. The series had reached Z and was to include a zoo owner, a zinc process worker and a zoologist; they were, however, short of a zinnia expert. Frances admitted to almost total ignorance on the subject of zinnias, but took part nevertheless and, thanks to slight confusion on the chairman's part, was questioned about plants, like the spelling of fuchsia. Her team not only won that round but went through to play against the 'A's in the finals and won the whole

Metasequoia glyptostroboides, **a deciduous conifer considered to be the oldest tree in the world. This one, planted in 1948, is one of the finest specimens in Britain.**

contest. She had taken the first step on the broadcasting path she was to walk so gracefully.

Her next advancement was caused by the resignation of her boss. There was a large field of applicants, all men, and at first Frances didn't even consider applying. Even when pressed to do so she demurred. There were no women in similar positions in the whole country, in any case she was married with small

children to look after. However, she was persuaded, put in an application and, to her amazement, was appointed. She was now the horticultural organiser for the whole county of Middlesex, the first woman to be appointed to such a position. Later, when the County Council formed a college of horticulture at Ealing, she became its principal. After she retired from teaching and organising, she became the first woman to be elected to the Council of the Royal Horticultural Society, later its first woman vice-president.

In an age where equal opportunity is at least attempted if not always accorded, the extent of Frances Perry's achievements perhaps needs stressing. When she started lecturing she was warned that she would have a fight, that people would say, 'What can a woman know about gardening?' and that she would have to be better than her male colleagues to be equal. She used to sit up night after night revising, making sure she would not get caught out by awkward questions. Gradually she saw women among the men in her audiences, saw the beginning of the garden clubs, which were closely allied to the Townswomen's Guilds, saw women take their place in the ranks of professional gardeners. Geoffrey Smith has remarked on the way she and Mary Spiller (one of the few other well-known professional woman gardeners of that generation) had the courage and confidence to remain themselves in a masculine world. Later generations of women are much in their debt.

Frances Perry has lived in the same house, at Bull's Cross near Enfield, for nearly half a century, so her half acre of garden is rather like a very large and exciting

Above, Asarum caudatum, of which Mr Bowles said, 'If the devil had a buttonhole, this is what he would wear.' Left, Frances Perry's unusual plants include the green-flowered Veratrum viride, which grows to a graceful four feet.

album of photographs; everywhere plants are reminders of people she has known, worked with, loved.

It has changed, of course. No doubt it will continue to change. When Gerald and Frances arrived the garden was swamped by an enormous beech tree; it wasn't until after the war, when the tree was felled, that work could really start. For many years Gerald developed it as a nursery garden, with rows of frames and lots of little beds; it was not until after his sudden death in 1964 that Frances began to make it her own. She had experienced bereavement before, nineteen years earlier, when she lost a child; she knew the value of work as therapy. In her distress she dug up nearly everything, planning, planting, finding some comfort in creation. She did not, in any case, want a garden that was half nursery, but 'a proper garden', by which she meant one broken up into borders, with a rockery, a pool, a vegetable patch, terraces, containers and lawn – but not too much, she finds the space is far too valuable for plants.

Frances considers herself primarily a plantswoman, interested in all plants, even those she does not grow, like tropical plants. In her extensive travels – she has visited seventy-eight countries – she always heads straight for any good private garden or, if there is one, the botanic garden. Her whole life is centred on plants; she grows them, she writes about them, she talks about them. They are, she says, her 'religion in life'.

Her taste is catholic and constantly changing, but she has her favourites. She attributes her love of old-fashioned roses, unusual bulbs, foliage plants, silver, variegated and herbaceous plants, largely to the influence of Mr Bowles and the Perrys. She is drawn to very small flowers – the sweet violet, the four-leaved clover, the tiny flowers of the threepenny bit rose, and 'that teeny arum, *Pinella ternata* – that gives me much more thrill than looking at great big plants.' She loves anything sweet-smelling, no doubt having a special warmth for the beautiful deep pink sweet pea that Unwins named after her.

Sometimes it is a whole family that is embraced with special affection. She has seven varieties of lily of the valley, including giant, pink, double flowered, and lilies of the valley with golden edged or striped leaves, and she knows no one who has more. She has a special fondness for poppies, almost synonymous with the name Perry. In 1903, when Amos Perry discovered a pink oriental poppy amongst the scarlet, it created a sensation. Nobody had ever seen a pink poppy before. He called it 'Mrs Perry' after his wife, Frances's mother-in-law. Though he did not succeed in his attempt to breed a white poppy, despite repeated crossings, ten years later he was the one to find it, in the border of a client, furious that his blaze of scarlet and pink had been spoilt by 'an intruder'. Amos rushed down to look at it, agreed that it was not, as he had thought it must be, an opium poppy, and named it 'Perry's White'. She also enjoys another member of the poppy family, *Meconopsis*, and was delighted to find, three years ago, a red Welsh poppy amongst the yellow and orange.

Despite her love of the small, one of her favourites is the largest tree in the garden, *Metasequoia glyptostroboides*, with its soft green feathery shoots turning to rosy crimson in the autumn. It is considered to be the oldest tree in the world and

Aruncus sylvester **and hydrangeas in a summer corner.**

was found in Western China in 1941 by three Chinese botanists. They didn't know it, they couldn't, no one had ever seen it, but they recognised its leaves from fossils. They collected seed, more expeditions were financed and it was introduced to Great Britain in 1947. Hillier's *Manual of Trees and Shrubs* says of it: 'The ease with which it is propagated and its rapid growth, plus its ornamental qualities, have combined to make this perhaps the most popular coniferous species in the shortest possible time. In this respect it has certainly beaten the potato "King Edward", the strawberry "Royal Sovereign" and the apple "Cox's Orange Pippin".' Frances is very proud of her specimen, given to her by Sir Harold Hillier the year after it was introduced and planted outside her conservatory by Gerald. With its lovely balanced shape right down to the ground, it is considered to be among the finest metasequoia in the country; Sir Eric Savill at Windsor once said that they had two hundred, but none so good as hers.

She also has her dislikes. She doesn't like annuals, though she makes an exception for the poached egg plant, *Limnanthes douglasii*. She hasn't much time for dahlias, is tired of seeing chrysanthemums forced to disregard the season and flower throughout the year, and she can't stand tagetes – the smell, the look, the stiffness. And water plants? The national expert on the subject might be expected to have a stunning water garden, but Frances has given hers up. She knows how much work they involve.

More and more it is the unusual plants that appeal to her now; plants which may not look very special – though often they do – but which are different, rare, freaky. She is particularly fond of the resin-scented *Asarum caudigerum*, of which Mr Bowles used to say, 'If the devil had a buttonhole, this is what he would wear', and other arums like the mouseplant, *Arum proboscideum* whose flowers burrow shyly beneath the leaves, invisible until sought out by an intrusive finger. When found, they resemble a mouse so closely that you expect them to run away.

The Royal Horticultural Society's *Dictionary of Gardening* considers *Smyrnium perfolatum* 'now no longer of horticultural interest', but Frances likes its yellow bracts, likes it, in any case, because apart from at Myddelton, she has never seen it anywhere else. Enjoying scents in the garden, she no doubt appreciates the smell of myrrh from which its name derives. Other favourites are *Veratrum viride*, whose yellow-green flowers can reach up to seven feet tall, and *Kirengeshoma palmata*, which produces yellow wax bells and tolerates deep shade. Mr Bowles's mint and Mr Bowles's black pansy would also always find a place, in memory of the man who started her on her gardening career.

Sometimes the unusual element is the shape. The corkscrew hazel, *Corylus avellana* 'Contorta', also known as Harry Lauder's walking stick, was found in a Gloucestershire hedgerow by Lord Ducie in 1863, who realised that he'd found a freak. It found its way to Bowles, who gave a layer to Frances. Apparently the seed which originally produced this strange plant had two dissimilar parents, one of which had a slow growing skin, the other a fast growing inside. These conflicting properties are the cause of the tree's contortions, resulting in corkscrew branches and curiously twisted leaves. It has a strange Japanese look, particularly in winter. Another strange shape, indeed another walking stick, comes from the fifteen-foot oddly named, because inedible, Jersey cabbage. In this essentially feminine garden the unusual includes the delicate, like the fern, *Athyrium filix-femina* 'Victoriae', found during the last century in Scotland and named after Queen Victoria because every part of every leaf is shaped like a 'V'.

Frances's sense of humour runs riot in her love of the unusual. The unwary visitor may be hit by the seeds of the squirting cucumber, *Ecballium elaterium*, as they are violently ejected from the ripe fruit; or stung by the hairy leaves of the *Loasa tricolor*. She has given up growing loasa, out of consideration for her friends, but she is not so easily kept from a peculiarly nasty arum, *Helicodiceros muscivorus*. It flowers in mid-June, a large flower, rather like a sow's ear with a rat's tail in the middle. 'For three days it stinks – there's no other word for it. People come and tell me that something's died in my garden. Then about mid-day it's smothered in blow flies, always green ones. They come from far and wide, obviously thinking it's bad meat. Everybody asks why I grow it. Well, I don't know, I just want it. I like it.' Be grateful that she only grows one. But she is threatening to start again with insectivorous plants.

One of the most remarkable plants in Frances's garden is a pink laburnum, *Laburnocytisus adamii*. It is a graft hybrid, with laburnum forming the core and broom the outer envelope, so the branches may carry yellow or pink laburnum,

Companion planting – Mr Bowles's wallflower set off by silver cardoon.

while sprays of broom come out of the trunk. Years ago they used to graft broom on laburnum to make a standard and this particular one went wrong in a garden in France in 1825. Frances's delight in the tree is increased by the knowledge that the garden where the tree originated belonged to a man called Adam.

Passionate though Frances's interest is in the plants for their own sake, she cares too about how they look in relation to each other, delighting in companion planting, whether accidental – the pink peony finding itself beside the blue hydrangea – or deliberate. She feels that people do not think enough about this side of gardening, admitting that it can only come with experience and intimate knowledge of the plants. Companion planting has much to do with colour and Frances prefers to see pinks, blues and reds together, keeping yellows, oranges and the autumnal colours in different places. She likes to set bright summer flowers against silver foliage, santolinas and lavenders; to have subtle combinations of blues and mauves. She doesn't agree with people who say that plants never clash, avoiding, for instance, brilliant scarlet and orange cheek by jowl, though she makes an exception for hanging baskets, feeling they should be spectacular and need no softening. Sometimes her groupings are in little families. She might have several varieties of lilies of the valley, all flowering at the same time, complementing each other; or in colours, the dusty purple sage growing with Mr Bowles's wallflower, with its brighter shade of mauve. She manages to have pleasing combinations throughout the year. For spring she has underplanted small pink cherry trees, *Prunus cerasifera* 'Rosea', with *Narcissus cyclamineus* and blue muscari; she still remembers a happy association one summer between a deep blue delphinium, 'Jack Tar', regale lilies and blue flax; the cream lily, touched with maroon at the base, the two slightly different blues of the delphinium and the flax combining in a way that pleased her greatly. In autumn there is a happy teaming of *Berberis thunbergii* 'Rose Glow', its purple leaves mottled with silver pink and bright rose, with the salmon pink *Sedum spectabile* 'Autumn Joy' and two Michaelmas daisies, the clear blue 'Climax' and the cerise pink 'Alma Potschke'.

Nine years ago Frances married again, another well-known gardener, Roy Hay. It could be difficult for two professional gardeners to work together in the same garden. Inevitably there are differences, Frances does not, for instance, share Roy's love of annuals and conifers. But Roy is quite clear on this. 'You don't have two head gardeners in one garden, especially when one of them is Frances Perry, looking after a garden she has put together painfully over forty-five years.' In any case, they are fortunate in that their interests compliment each other very happily, Roy looking after the equipment, the grass, the greenhouse and a few annuals, while Frances concentrates on the plants. She also does most of the weeding – all handweeding. She won't use weedkillers because they are too indiscriminate, and you don't, as she says, 'get any volunteers coming up'.

It was through Bowles that Frances came to be interested in plants' backgrounds, where they come from, their scientific properties, how they were

Corkscrew hazel, also known as Harry Lauder's walking stick. This plant started as a layer from the original freak found in Gloucestershire over a hundred years ago.

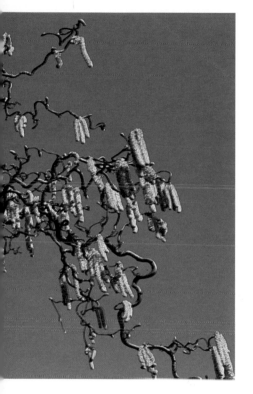

introduced, what Roy calls 'the story behind the label'. As a child, she and her friends sometimes sheltered during a storm with Bowles under the great gunnera that Gerald Perry's grandfather had planted at Myddelton House. Its leaves could be as much as six feet across. Bowles would tell the children how a man from Ecuador, where the gunnera grows wild, had claimed that they grew even larger in South America, so large, in fact, that he had seen a man on horseback standing under one of the leaves. However the South American's bluff was called when he said he had never seen a larger plant than the one at Myddelton. Bowles reminded him of his boast. 'Oh yes,' he said, 'I did say that, but it was a very small man and it was only a pony.' Then Bowles would cut a leaf off and use it as an umbrella as the little group returned to the house.

Now Frances has collected many stories, adding a magical, legendary quality to her garden. Her cistus plants remind her of Napoleon, who reputedly claimed that he could recognise his native Corsica with his eyes shut, simply from the scent of these plants. This scent is due to a sticky aromatic gum on the foliage known as ladanum, which has been gathered since time immemorial for its spicy fragrance. The ladanum was collected by driving goats through the shrubs, then raking their hair with combs of untanned hide. The beards of the goats, heavily impregnated with the scented gum, were severed and worn as false beards by the Pharaohs. The original 'goatee' perhaps? The ancient Egyptians were particularly attracted to fragrant plants, indeed the world's first plant collector, Queen Hatshepsut of Egypt, sent collectors to 'the land of Punt' (now the Somali Republic) in search of incense-scented boswellia trees, the frankincense of the Bible.

Many flower legends have a religious basis. Frances will tell visitors to her garden of the *Fritillaria imperialis*, the crown imperial, whose flowers were once upon a time white and looked upwards. The legend has it that this flower was growing in the Garden of Gethsemane when Our Lord passed through. At his passing all the flowers hung their heads in humility, save this one, with its crown of leaves, too proud to bow. So Our Lord rebuked it, at which it hung its head in shame, blushed a rosy red and tears came into its eyes. Turning up the leaves reveals the drops of nectar, which cannot be shaken off; even when absorbed by blotting paper they are soon replaced. The plant has, says Frances, one failing – a strong foxy smell, once described by Bowles as 'a mixture of mangy fox, dirty dog kennel, the small cats' house at the zoo and Exeter railway station'.

It would be a mistake to be lured by the romance of these legends into thinking Frances Perry is a gardener with her head in the clouds. She is not. No one reaches her position in the horticultural élite without getting their hands dirty. In fact this, to Frances, is one of the attractions of gardening. Her garden is both an outdoor room of the house, which she can change around as she does her home, live in, sit and enjoy, and a place where she can handle plants, get her hands in the soil, be busy and active, or just stand and stare. Much of the joy of gardening is in its combination of activity and stillness, hard work and fantasy, technology and mystery. 'People talk a lot about green fingers, but when you get down to it, it's black knees and black fingernails that really count.'

BILL SOWERBUTTS

FROM BRUSSELS SPROUTS TO LOOFAHS

BILL Sowerbutts has been gardening since he was six years old, not so much from love as from necessity. He was one of five children born to a market gardener in Ashton-under-Lyne, who, as soon as they were old enough to be useful, were pressed into service. There is a Dickensian flavour to the thought of these small boys fetching and carrying, filling pots with soil, wheeling barrows, picking frozen sprouts on a cold January morning. It was not a question of whether they enjoyed it or not; this was soon after the first world war, when parents were obeyed, not questioned.

Commercial gardening is a far cry from gardening in private service or in a parks department. It's a deadly serious business and a tough one. Produce has to be sold, at a profit, or the bailiffs will be at the door. Not only is quantity essential and the highest quality desirable, the commercial grower is at the whim of the seasons and his customers. While the retailer can change direction in a day or so, the producer can take anything from a year, in the case of annual crops, to two or three, in the case of fruit, before he is ready to respond to a change in the market. For many in those days market gardening was a family business. Traditionally the women, considered to be better with money and to have more sense anyway, went to market to sell the produce, while the men stopped at home to do the growing.

Bill did not intend to pursue a lifetime of gardening. As the youngest of the Sowerbutts children he profited from his father's hard work and improved fortunes and went on to higher education, unlike his elder brothers and sister, who left school at fourteen to work in the family business. He had been interviewed by the local paper and was set for a career in journalism when, very quickly and suddenly, his father died of cancer of the thyroid. So at only sixteen his hopes were dashed; he had to forget about higher education and join his brothers in the market garden.

Apart from a little botany at school, his training was practical and pragmatic. He had learnt a good deal from his father, he continued learning from experience, by making mistakes, by testing the market, most of all by sheer hard

A view across the valley to the distant Pennines with *Berberis stenophylla* in flower, and a columnar yew in the foreground.

work. The soil was good black mossland, providing excellent conditions for their basic crop, celery. They grew vast quantities of celery, in rows four feet apart, interplanted with cauliflowers, lettuce, both cabbage and cos, radishes and spring onions. They needed to persuade their twelve acres to yield bountifully.

In the greenhouses they grew cucumbers, melons, tomatoes, cyclamen, geraniums; outdoors there were cut flowers – peonies, scabious, asters, nemesias, stocks. Old Mr Sowerbutts, a wonderful gardener, had allowed himself to be tempted into growing the cinerarias and calceolarias that he loved, but his children had seen them flower and remain unsold and had learnt to grow only what the public wanted, not what they felt like growing.

Above, the lake with flag iris, overhung by azalea and an ancient copper beech; *right,* a fine weeping elm and honeysuckle azalea grace the old tennis court.

Bill turned out to have a taste for commerce, loving the market place, getting a thrill from buying for five pence and selling for ten. He was also ambitious, independent and impatient – his own word is pig-headed. 'I wanted to run before I could walk. I wanted to go out in my own little boat and row it, and hopefully not to sink.' It must have been galling for him when the next-door nursery came up for sale and his mother bought it for one of his elder brothers. But his Lancashire grit and determination showed early. In his spare time he did up old cars – Austin Sevens, Peugeots, Fords – anything on four wheels that he could buy for ten pound and sell for twenty. Soon he had enough money to rent some land and buy a place in Ashton market from his brother, who had not been doing too well, despite the start he had been given. For some time the cars were his main money-spinner, but gradually the market gardening grew and flourished, until at its peak he was employing over forty people. He was to start branches in Manchester, London, Warrington, Hyde and Rochdale, providing himself with work and income for fifty years, in fact until he sold the business in 1980.

Above, one of the finest English elms in the district, saved from Dutch elm disease by timely injections; *right, Rhododendron* 'Pink Pearl'.

'What do you do with a barrow-load of steel? Do you make a railway bridge or a million safety pins?' It soon became obvious to Bill that he must adapt his business to the fluctuations imposed by a seasonal trade. The gardening world is always busy in spring and early summer, but come the cold months of winter and not only are gardeners short of work, they are likely to be short of money as well. A million safety pins makes good commercial sense when translated into horticultural terms, so he developed three separate businesses. He continued and expanded the growing of vegetables, he added a section growing expensive salads of the highest quality, he spread the cut flowers into floristry, making wreaths and posies and becoming a member of Interflora. This was good for business because he was never without something to sell; it also gave him the flexibility to move staff around from one section to another according to the need. There were no Trade Unions, so he was not restricted by rules and regulations.

Learning, as Bill did, through hard experience, one would not expect him to be distracted by theory. For instance his common sense does not allow him to tangle with the pros and cons of organic gardening; for him the marriage between chemical and organic methods is a happy one. While, like any good gardener, he puts the health of the soil firmly first, he relies little on chemical fertilisers, feeling that soil health can be assured with lashings of manure and compost. However it is not always possible to get enough and if you are growing to sell, you cannot be romantic; so he accepts that for the commercial grower, and indeed for the amateur, synthetic fertilisers are inseparable from good crops. He also believes that the few natural insecticides and the even fewer natural fungicides are simply not good enough when there are more effective ones available. 'If people have pneumonia we use streptomycin or something like that. We don't get the steam kettle out these days or plaster the chest with antiphlogistine. To me it's just as simple and just as sensible as that.'

The place – the singing room of the Broadoak Hotel, Ashton-under-Lyne. The year – 1947. Alan Faulkner, Parks Superintendent of Ashton-under-Lyne, Fred Loads, Tom Clarke, Parks Superintendent of Bolton, and Bill Sowerbutts, market gardener, are gathered together under the chairmanship of a young BBC producer, Robert Stead. Their audience – the Smallshaw Gardening Society. Listeners to the BBC's North of England service are about to hear *How Does Your Garden Grow?* and broadcasting history is being made. Thirty-eight years later the programme, now known as *Gardeners' Question Time* and the BBC's longest running talks programme, draws a weekly audience of approaching two million listeners; it has visited over 1600 gardening clubs, answered at least 200,000 questions and established professional gardeners as national figures. Bill Sowerbutts is the one surviving member of that original team, only leaving the programme in 1983.

The history of this remarkable programme goes back to the beginning of the second world war. Many people, still with memories of the food shortages of the 1914–18 war, realised that the same situation was certain to arise again. ICI, who had invested heavily in the garden chemical market, decided to send

Gloxinia and campanula in the heated greenhouse.

An azalea flowering as the daffodils fade.

representatives round the country, briefed to visit horticultural societies and encourage people to grow their own produce. It was part of the 'Dig For Victory' campaign. Many will still remember its poster, the booted foot bearing down on the spade.

The area representative knew Bill, who was invited to share his knowledge of commercial growing. So all through the war, he, with a small team, travelled around northern cities and towns such as Ashton, Oldham, Rochdale, Manchester, Huddersfield and Bradford; they visited pubs, church halls – anywhere where twenty or thirty people could gather together – giving advice, answering questions, encouraging, no doubt entertaining as well. When Robert Stead, seeing the potential of outside broadcasts, decided to take his microphones to the gardeners, it was with this already established team that he began.

Soon the programme was transmitted nationally, every Sunday at two o'clock. Bill, already with an enviable reputation for imparting advice to small groups, became a name and a voice respected by hundreds of thousands of amateur gardeners. He took to broadcasting like a fish to swimming. 'I was only doing what came naturally, I could almost do it in my sleep.'

By 1950, with the arrival of Professor (then Dr) Alan Gemmell, the programme had found the team it was to keep for an astonishing thirty-three years, the third member being the much-loved Fred Loads. Fred had spent much of his working life in private service, where he was presented with particular challenges like having to produce fruit and vegetables all the year round; being

Streptocarpus '**Concorde**' **and** *Begonia* '**Gloire de Lorraine**'.

sure to have a rose for the Duke's button hole every morning; growing onions in India or tomatoes in Iraq. Bill provided the practical, cost-conscious advice, applying commercial practices of proved value to the home gardener, while Alan Gemmell, the scientist, balanced their knowledge of *how* to do things with his understanding of *why* they should be done that way. They made a trio as well-matched as a mixed grill, complementing each other both in knowledge and in manner. Their success lay largely in the way they seasoned their information with a human, entertaining approach. They teased, parried, persuaded, cajoled, argued, took every opportunity to make a joke or even to stage a row. It was all in good part. In private life they were the best of friends, appreciating how much they learnt from each other. Their easy relationship allowed them to stretch their badinage to the limit. On one occasion Alan Gemmell, who admits that at first he didn't know much about the growing of plants, was dubbed by Bill 'The Professor of Horticultural Malpractice'. He got away with it.

Bill does not expect everyone to appreciate his deadpan, Lancastrian humour, but though he is at pains to conceal his good-natured heart, he doesn't quite succeed. His tact enables him to sail, quite safely, very close to the wind. 'Sometimes it is a risk. For instance, I might feel like saying to a lady who wanted to prune a large apple tree but was fearful of climbing a ladder, "Aren't you married?" That won't do, she might have lost her husband last week. On the other hand, if it's someone with sparkling eyes you could play ball with, you might say, "Get your husband to prune it." If she said she wasn't married I would say "Not married, a lovely girl like you? I could fix that for a small fee." '

Behind all the banter there was, of course, a deep reservoir of knowledge. As in a doctor's surgery, it was often the same problems that came up – reminding the owner of a wilting saintpaulia that the foliage must not be allowed to become wet, unveiling the mysteries of club root disease, advising on the right time to prune a plum tree. But sometimes the questions were more obscure, like the one from a lady who planted Russell lupins, which should be bi-coloured or tri-coloured, but which one year confounded her by all coming up blue. Bill had the explanation. 'The parent plant dies, but sheds seeds which have reverted to the original. The parent hasn't turned blue at all, it has just died, but the seed it shed has changed character genetically.' You would need to have a good horticultural library to have question like that answered so clearly.

Broadcasting had its spin-offs for Bill as for many others. *Gardeners' Question Time* had not been running for two years before he was approached by the Northern Editor of the *Sunday Graphic*. Would he write a weekly gardening column, about 300 words, at ten pounds a time? At last he could do what he set out to do twenty years earlier. He was so popular that his column went national and the fee was trebled. However, his success as a journalist was greater than his luck in choosing his outlets. The *Sunday Graphic,* the *Daily Sketch* and the *Manchester Evening Chronicle* all folded soon after his arrival on their pages. He likes to boast that he has closed more newspapers than anyone else he knows.

Though Bill is indifferent to the challenge of writing books – he has only accepted one approach, and this he filled with a collection of already published articles – his love of journalism has never left him. At seventy-four he still writes a syndicated gardening column for about fifty provincial newspapers, as far north as Galloway, as far south as Plymouth. The articles must follow the variations in latitude, so he has to be sensitive to gardening conditions all over the country, writing about soft fruits for Galloway, where apples and plums do not grow very well, while he is covering hard fruits for the more favourable conditions of Exeter and Malvern. Typically he does not let a syndication agency take their percentage, but Joan Rigby, his secretary for thirty years, rings round and sells directly to the papers. 'This is the individual pig-headed streak in me again. I hate paying Mr Ten Per Cent or Mr Twenty Per Cent, even though I realise that in some cases they can earn you more than you are paying them. But I also know that the reverse can happen.'

Unlike many gardening correspondents he encourages letters, finding the work involved very rewarding. The number of queries varies with the seasons, as in all things horticultural, but he seldom receives less than a hundred letters a week and he answers each one personally.

With his background of obligatory gardening, his associations of hard, unremitting work, it is little surprise that gardening is not high on Bill Sowerbutts' priorities when it comes to his leisure time. In fact for years he would not have called it one of his hobbies at all. He prefers golf and music – he

Above, the heated greenhouse in August; *right,* the breakfast tomato developed and grown by Bill Sowerbutts, who considers it ugly and uncommercial but likes the flavour.

calls himself a 'reasonable' classical pianist – and on a desert island would prefer a piano to a spade. He also enjoys cricket, proud of the century he scored at Glossop in 1935 and amused to remember that as Captain of Crompton he once had Learie Constantine in his team. His brief moment of power over this great cricketer meant more to him than had he borrowed Gertrude Jekyll's services as an under gardener.

Why then, when house-hunting thirty years ago, did he settle for a large house and thirty acres of land? The answer reflects the man – a shrewd businessman with a strong, if not an obvious, romantic streak. He liked the setting, the view over the hills, the trees and the open space, but he liked them even more when he realised that it was a good commercial proposition. For some years much of the land was an extension of his business and, with the help of two gardeners, he grew cut flowers, dahlias, gladioli, chrysanthemums and peonies, only giving up when local pilfering and vandalism made it impossible to continue. Despite this curtailment of a proper and good use of land, he is about to reap unforeseen commercial benefit, as he is negotiating to sell most of it to the local authority. He could not get permission to build on it, so the plan is that it should be used as a wildlife park. He will keep an acre round the house and will have a key to the other twenty-nine, so as he gets older he will be able to enjoy the trees and the open space without being responsible for their upkeep.

The twenty-nine acres with which he is parting will make a beautiful wildlife park, perhaps helping the local youth to appreciate their environment rather than destroying it. At present it is an informal garden ('I hate formal gardens, French

style with parterres and all that nonsense') laid out by a professional over a hundred years ago. Much of it is woodland, the house crowning the highest point, giving dramatic views over the tops of the trees to the Pennines beyond. It is full of bulbs, rhododendrons and azaleas and Bill regards it as essentially a spring garden. But the trees make a sight to lift the spirit at any season of the year. There is a particularly graceful weeping elm, maples, larches, flagpole cherries, match poplars, a weeping ash and a truly magnificent English elm, probably the finest in the district, which Bill had the foresight to save from Dutch elm disease by timely injections. Deep down in the woodland, surrounded by yet more trees, including a copper beech, is a small lake, planted with water lilies and inhabited by mallard, trout and water hens.

Bill is a humble and rather pessimistic gardener, tending to say that there's nothing very interesting out just now, the camellia's over the top, the bulbs are finished, the campanulas haven't flowered yet, pointing out weeds, a tree with beetle, holes where the rabbits have been at work. One must look at the garden, rather than listen to the gardener, to see what it has to offer.

He has added many plants and shrubs to his inheritance of trees. Liking masses of colour he has planted in big, bold groups – he feels that shows the commercial streak in him. Near the house is a group of azaleas, mixed with about ten different kinds of berberis, which grow in grass and seed themselves abundantly. He likes berberis partly because they are tough and his garden, cowering under the Pennines, is cold and wet. There are borders of hypericum and potentilla, a hedge of red flowering currant mixed with yellow forsythia, a group of weigela. There were rhododendrons, modern varieties which he had planted, but many of them were stolen. Understandably enough he has lost heart and stopped planting them. The area that was used commercially is now a mass of shrub roses – rugosas, bourbons, damask. Even though, with the sale imminent, he is no longer doing much with the land, there are splendid vistas, much evidence of good gardening.

Nothing and nobody compels Bill Sowerbutts to garden any longer, no parental pressure, no commercial obligation. His business sold, most of his land soon to be cared for by the local authority, he could feel justified in putting his feet up and giving his time to spectator sports, music, simply doing nothing. But the desire to grow plants, once kindled, does not die down easily. At last he is free to garden or not to garden, as he chooses. 'Now I can grow what I like, when I like, if I like.'

The restraints of professional gardening lifted, where does his fancy take him? Does he grow huge exhibition dahlias? Cultivate a lawn like green baize? Enjoy the miniature delights of alpines, with their kindness to both backs and space? Despite a splendid display of trees and shrubs round the house – climbing hydrangea, magnolia and *Garrya elliptica* – he is not too interested in outdoor gardening now. His pleasure lies in the greenhouse, where he can be dry in all weathers, where there is virtually no bending and, most of all, where his frustrated romanticism can find expression.

He has three greenhouses, two unheated and one heated. There is an unheated

Bill Sowerbutts pollinating his loofahs, a regular supply of original Christmas presents.

lean-to on the south-facing back of the house where he grows vines (he has just replaced one that developed the root disease to which they are prone), mimosa, fuchsias, a *Kalmia latifolia*, also known as the calico bush, geraniums, camellias, a bread-fruit tree (the fruit forms the staple diet of the Pacific Islanders), potatoes started in heat and grown on in eight and a half-inch pots and a tender member of the pea family, *Erythrina crista-galli*, the coral tree from Brazil. An important point for visitors – the sliding door must be kept open, but not too far; it must be just wide enough for the cat to get in and deal with the mice, narrow enough to keep the hen out.

In the front garden there is another unheated lean-to, facing due west. This he has filled with many of the same plants, though being colder they flower three weeks or so later. He loves scented flowers, considering himself fortunate, in view of his continual pipe-smoking, to retain a keen sense of smell, so there are also hyacinths, scented narcissus and scented tulips, like the bright orange 'Prince of Austria'.

His real pleasure, pleasure of pleasures, is in the heated greenhouse; a few square feet of his Pennine village transformed into a mediterranean paradise. He keeps it heated to a minimum of 60°F and in summer it can reach 110°F. He loves to walk into the warm air on a cold winter morning when it could be 25°F outside. There he grows what he calls 'sub-tropicals' – oleander, bougainvillaea, brunfelsia, gynura (the purple-leaved passion flower) and *Crassula argentea*, the money plant. His wife makes marmalade with the fruits they gather from the miniature orange, *Citrus mitis*; they eat pomegranates from their own bushes,

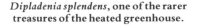

Dipladenia splendens, **one of the rarer treasures of the heated greenhouse.**

kept to a reasonable size by growing them by the Bonsai method; he grows several varieties of tomato, including one that he developed himself twenty years ago. Ugly, he feels, and not a heavy enough cropper to be used commercially, but he likes the flavour and is clearly proud of it. So he should be.

There is something colourful and interesting the year round, but perhaps its peak is in July, when it is a mass of campanula, gloxinia and rarer treasures like *Dipladenia splendens* and the delicate wax flower *Hoya carnosa*. But if the pride of the garden is the heated greenhouse, then surely the pride of the greenhouse must be one of the most unusual plants to be grown in the whole of Lancashire. It is *Luffa cylindrica*, the bathroom loofah. The loofah is a member of the cucurbit family and like its cousins, the marrows and the melons, the female flower has to be fertilised with the pollen from the male. The fruit cannot be eaten but the fibrous interior is used to scrub bathing backs. It need hardly be said that he grows them successfully, so successfully that he uses them himself, gives them away to friends and grows next year's crop from his own seeds.

Gardening for Bill is now a relaxed, pleasurable hobby, a lifetime away from picking frozen brussels sprouts on a cold winter morning. He has help to mow the lawn, he doesn't worry too much if he doesn't get around to dead-heading the camellias or netting the lettuce to prevent the hen from uprooting them. (She tends to favour the stone sink, where for some reason they are grown, for her dust bath.) Gardening is not an obsession for him, no longer a necessity, but a skill that brings its own gentle pleasures in just the way he chooses. What gardener would not delight in producing a two-foot loofah?

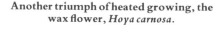

Another triumph of heated growing, the wax flower, *Hoya carnosa*.

ALAN TITCHMARSH

A GAY ABANDON

IS Alan Titchmarsh mad or is he a masochist? Friends who watched as he moved into his new house in Hampshire may be forgiven for wondering. In 1982 he and his wife Alison found a house they liked near Alton; it had an acre and a third of land which had not seen a spade in years. Though virgin territory is a challenge to most gardeners, this inhospitable corner of Hampshire would surely have daunted all but the bravest. It is a long, thin strip, an eighth of a mile long and a hundred feet wide; the soil is clay, flint and chalk; it rises thirty feet up a cold, north-facing slope. All the initial cultivation had to be done with a fork or even a pick, as nothing else would go into the neglected soil until it had been worked over at least once. Surely nobody in their right mind would make a garden there?

In fact Alan Titchmarsh is very much in his right mind and he has his reasons. As a professional gardener, keen to communicate his enthusiasm, he needs to have first-hand experience of all gardening problems. If he had ideal conditions, with rich, friable soil like brown velvet in which he could sink his arm up to the elbow, people might feel it was easy enough for him, but how could they follow his example with their soil, conditions, wind or climate? 'I thought that if I had a garden where the conditions were absolutely dreadful and everything was against me, then anything I could do or grow in it, anybody else could do.' An unusual attitude – imagine John McEnroe choosing a badly strung racquet for Wimbledon – but persuasive.

Alan Titchmarsh has a vigorous, joyful approach to gardening, a passion that has been with him since he was a toddler. He still vividly remembers his grandfather's allotment, with blackberries growing over a brass bedstead and its great tank of soot water, used as a spray against blackfly. He treasures a photograph of his grandfather holding his hand as they walk together through a

Two years' hard work and already the garden begins to take shape. The *Catalpa bignonioides* 'Aurea' will become a distinctive and permanent feature. The annuals provide instant colour.

row of peas, garlanded with Cadbury's chocolate tins to frighten off the birds. A few years later he was leaving his friends playing football while he planted annuals in a corner of his parents' garden in Yorkshire. He feels, perhaps like many born gardeners, that he has sap running through his veins instead of blood.

His parents encouraged him, though wondering privately whether his enthusiasm would last, so at fifteen, he joined the Ilkley Urban District Council Parks Department. He had left school under a bit of a cloud, with only one 'O' level, his confidence as frail as his passion for plants was strong. He could hardly believe that he was being paid for doing what he most enjoyed.

Propagating 15,000 geraniums didn't deter him (or kill his love of geraniums) and he impressed his employers sufficiently for them to feel that, having had a five-year apprenticeship, he should go to college. A year later, armed with a Certificate of Horticulture from Oaklands, the Hertfordshire College of Agriculture and Horticulture, he went on to the Royal Botanic Gardens at Kew to study for the diploma. Six months of his time there were spent in the Palm House, where he was casually told to look after some strange primitive plants, the like of which he had never seen before. He was more than a little intimidated when he discovered that one of them was a rare cycad, collected by Captain Cook in 1776.

The first corner of the garden to be completed was the patio, specially designed for television.

There's nothing like doing what one wants to bring out one's best. His feeling of being a duffer lessened when he was awarded the trophy for being the best academic student of his year, disappearing completely when he was invited on to the staff as supervisor of staff training.

The three-year diploma course had given him a varied education in botany, plant classification, the study of fungi and insects, landscape design, arboriculture. There were some subjects he found boring, like management; many more that he thrilled to, like growing plants from all over the world – alpines and tropicals, slow growing conifers, giant bamboos that reached the roof of the Palm House in a few weeks. After a couple of years in staff training he was tempted into journalism, first as a gardening books editor, then on to the editorial staff of *Amateur Gardening*. It was while he was there that he was asked to do his first broadcast. Would he like to do a piece on turfing for the BBC radio programme, *You and Yours*? He would, he did, he was a success.

Media careers are often built on the unexpected. For Alan Titchmarsh the first steps to television fame were a greenfly invasion in Margate and a collapsing roof garden in Fulham. His broadcast advice on these subjects led to a five-year stint on *Nationwide*, then to becoming *Breakfast Time*'s resident gardener.

So, in 1979, against all advice, his wife expecting their first child, he went

freelance. His life now consists of writing, both books and journalism, broadcasting and working in his own garden. He hasn't for one moment regretted his decision.

The herb garden, cultivated as much for fun as gastronomic delight.

The Titchmarshes' first home was a town house with a tiny garden fifteen feet by forty, so he knows both the frustrations and the miniature delights of a small garden. 'I used a shoe horn to plant it, not a trowel. You could almost hear the plants fighting for space.' Space is no longer a problem, but he faces new challenges, which he tackles with a breezy confidence. His approach is epitomised by the way he deals with the inevitable soil erosion. 'It's not too bad. The soil washes down a bit, I just kick it back and put some more on.'

The third of an acre near the house, the part under most cultivation is – it would be, of course – the north-facing slope. (The top flattens out into an acre of paddock.) There was not much there when they moved in; a few very old, gnarled fruit trees, a damson hedge, raspberry canes full of mosaic disease, tree stumps and two weed-infested stony borders. This was his inheritance, his skeleton. Most people would call it flimsy or worse. He calls it useful.

The first year he sat back and watched. Perhaps dormant delights would unfold before his eyes? In any case he was obeying the first rule for anyone taking over a new garden – wait and see. He saw snowdrops, then daffodils, peonies and poppies. There were poppies everywhere, not just in the weedy patches pretending to be borders, but coming through the lawn, round the roots of trees, struggling through nettles. He saw the seasons round, then he began to plan.

He never works from paper, but plans the garden from the ground and from the upstairs windows. He's had two little dormer windows built on the back of the house to give him a good view over the garden. Then he sculpts on the soil, drawing lines for the outlines of borders, tracing in paths, marking with sticks the places where there will, one day, be trees.

Given Alan's exuberant, creative temperament, it is no surprise that his garden is a mosaic of little rooms and areas, gardens within a garden, each one reflecting some different passion, interest, need. Gardens can reflect their owners, become like them.

As his land falls naturally into two areas, the children are not restricted by their father's botanical zeal. They learn young to keep off the beds, but have the run of the paddock. Here the Titchmarshes inherited a dozen mature oaks, a few hawthorns, a venerable birch, at nearly eighty years old somewhat past its best, plenty of nettles and a horse, which somehow got left behind with the fixtures and fittings, remaining for their first three months and leaving a legacy of hoofprints and tattered turf. Alan wants to keep this area wild, so apart from planting a few ornamental trees – a davidia, or pocket handkerchief tree, has pride of place – and a cluster of dogwoods, its purpose is to encourage wildlife. There are bluebells, primroses, solomon's seal; a host of butterflies emerge every year and the birds are provided with nesting boxes if they don't favour the trees. It is also intended to be a place of relaxation for the family with their different needs. The children have a wonderland for hide-and-seek and fantasy, to which Alan has added a tree-house. His wife can retire to the summer house at the top of the paddock (known as 'the Far Pavilion') when the television cameras take over the lower part of the garden on their weekly visit. He has his own favourite perch, sitting in one of the oak trees, five hundred feet above sea level, watching the deer in the neighbouring field and looking over towards Selborne, home of the naturalist Gilbert White.

The first part of the garden to be completed was, it had to be, the little patio regularly used for Breakfast Television. It is just outside the kitchen door, an area about twenty-four-feet square, rough ground when he took over, now immaculate. Indeed it is so immaculate that Alan, who prefers what he calls a gay abandon with plants spilling naturally through each other, seems mildly embarrassed by its perfection. There is crazy paving underfoot; a seat, backed by a trellis festooned with vines and clematis; a few small borders, filled with a framework of shrubs interplanted with annuals. The emphasis here is on colour, carefully blended and graded. In one border there are white cistuses and campanulas, pink mallow and blue nemophila; in another white flowered hebes and a yellow-variegated dogwood. Late-flowering lilies and everlasting flowers for drying extend the season. Hostas and bamboos grow in a shady corner; *Raoulia australis, Houstonia caerulea* ('a real smasher') and dwarf conifers in a small stone sink, while height is provided by what will one day be a statuesque *Gleditsia triacanthos* 'Sunburst'. A patio would not be complete without a few pots. Alan ensures strong bushy pelargoniums by using large pots, a minimum of ten inches in diameter, so that the plants do not dry out on the hot paving. He grows a spectacular variety 'Golden Crest', with deep pink flowers and golden leaves, slightly frilly round the edges.

Next to be tackled was the area visible from the kitchen sink, that part of the garden with which considerate designers take especial care. Alan dislikes bare walls, appreciating their potential as a host for climbers, so a fuchsia-flowered gooseberry, *Ribes speciosum*, nods round the window in spring, followed by a clematis, *C. viticella*, which grows through its branches and flowers from July till September.

The long slope up the garden starts under the windows with a rock bank, originally full of malmstone, a compact, chalky clay, now into its third year and beginning to please its creator. So it should. It is planted with a few dwarf conifers, though not too many, as Alan finds them funereal, rock roses, the much under-used miniature willows, several varieties of acaena – you need to look closely to see one of the best, the miniature bronzy-green *A. microphylla* – and pentstemons. His favourite variety is 'Garnet', for its intense wine-crimson colour and long flowering season. He finds that every year one or two plants succumb to the winter – a tender hebe perhaps, but he treats this philosophically, on the whole keeping the plants that are clearly happy, not persisting too long with unwilling performers.

To stroll round Alan Titchmarsh's garden, or perhaps one should say to climb up it, is to be continually delighted. A zig-zag path wanders past borders, banks, a herb garden, a vegetable patch; through formality and informality, 'gay abandon' and graceful symmetry; past areas that are as nearly completed as anything in a garden ever is, areas under development, areas not yet fully planned. He doesn't see himself as a plantsman, interested above all in collecting plants but fairly indifferent to where they are in relation to each other. 'It's not a stable, the garden. It's an art gallery where it's just as important how the pictures are hung as what pictures they are.' His approach is, indeed, as much artistic as horticultural. Art was his best subject at school (his one 'O' level, in fact) and his great pleasure is in painting and sculpting with plants. He is impressed by the architect Sir Frederick Gibberd, who claimed that gardening is the most complicated art form, because you are dealing not only with colour, form and texture, but also with time. Further, time in the garden is of two kinds, seasonal time, with the changes throughout the twelve months, and time across the years, as plants grow and develop.

Painting with plants. In this corner Alan Titchmarsh sees his idea taking shape.

The gardener who aspires to be an artist must not only be able to ensure his plants' good health, but must know them so intimately that he can place them skilfully, one enhancing the other. The choice can spear the chooser on the horns of one horticultural dilemma after another, with bewildering considerations of colours, height, spread, time and length of flowering, texture, habit and growing conditions jostling for attention. In three years Alan is only satisfied with a few of his living pictures. One is an enchanting combination of the hybrid musk rose 'Buff Beauty' and *Cotinus coggygria*, the pale cinnamon of the rose being deliciously set off by the purple leaves of the smoke bush. Another is a larger group, mainly yellow, with touches of pink and purple. Here the variegated box elder, *Acer negundo* 'Variegatum', with its green leaves edged with creamy white, stands among two old-fashioned roses, a pink and a purple, the yellow *Physocarpus opulifolius* 'Dart's Gold' and a purple-leaved berberis, *B. ottawensis* 'Superba'. The colours are carried down with clumps of dark purple mourning widow geranium, *(G. phaeum)*, and the flat-headed *Achillea* 'Gold Plate.' An inspired contrast of texture is given by the addition of the feather grass, *Stipa gigantea*, whose oat-laden plumes turn to shiny gold as they ripen. Here the partnership between artist and gardener is seen at its most successful.

Alan's aim is not only to have plants in groups that please him, but that they should be part of interlocking vistas, with focal points to draw and rest the eye. So one vista pivots round two stones, (called Jack and Jill because they took so long to get up the hill); another on a few poles that his wife calls 'the four-poster' but which Alan insists is a gazebo and intends to cover with roses and clematis; he plans to centre another on an old beehive. Sometimes the main feature is provided by a plant – a particularly striking rowan, a poplar, *P. candicans* 'Aurora', though now he feels this is off centre, or an acer, kept in a stone pot while it is small to ensure its dominance. Even pots to force rhubarb and sea kale are incorporated into the design as bits of sculpture.

The element of the unexpected continues into the vegetable patch. Alan likes vegetables to look good in the ground as well as to taste good, so both the manner of growing and the choice of varieties is taken seriously. He grows them in three-foot squares in the French *potager* style, so that the effect is something like a patchwork quilt. This not only looks charming, it has practical advantages. 'It's more convenient than long rows, because if you feel like a five-minute blitz, you can do a square, instead of being faced with a long row and not getting round to it.' He grows many of the predictable vegetables and, typically, some surprises, like the red-leaved Italian lettuce and a purple-podded pea. The peas themselves are still green, the taste is not very different, so, sadly, this joke doesn't reach the table.

In the herb garden, surrounded by its tiny yew hedge as neat as the line on a guardsman's trousers, Alan indulges his love for occasional formality. The circle with paths to east and west, edged with bricks and filled with gravel is, in design, reminiscent of a Celtic cross. Around it grows sorrel, curry plant, purslane, variegated nasturtium, marjoram, dill, feverfew, pot marigold, chervil, borage and both eau de cologne and ginger mint – a choice to delight the most inventive

cook, though Alan is motivated more by the sheer fun of growing them than by the promise of gastronomic pleasures.

In fact it is this sense of fun that permeates Alan Titchmarsh's garden. It bubbles up all over the place, from the gazebo to the beehive; to an old grindstone turned into a water feature. There's a chamomile seat, made the old English way, by planting a brick table bed filled with earth; it provides a sweet-smelling seat to rest on halfway up the hill. The fun continues in his choice of plants. He grows a variegated knotweed, amused by its leaves 'looking like some revolting cheese'; ostrich ferns for their sculptural, shuttlecock shape; *Pentstemon* 'Sour Grapes' for its name. His future plans include turning a daunting bed of nettles into a maze. This garden is a glorious kaleidoscope of botanical fun; an expression of creative personality with its roots, for the most part, firmly in the earth.

Alan clearly finds it hard to curb his creativity, but he knows all too well that fun in a garden involves hard work; he tries to stay on the right side of good sense, keeping his garden as a pleasure, refusing to let it become a millstone. But the line between good stewardship of the land and excessive worrying is a fine one. Though in theory he feels that gardening should be like fishing, where half

Left, an old grindstone turned into a water feature; *above,* the vegetable garden, designed on the French *potager* style, includes red-leaved lettuce.

the pleasure is sitting on the bank doing nothing, in practice he has to be numbered with countless gardeners, both amateur, and professional, who are drawn out of their chairs by the demanding magnetism of a weed, lettuces that should be watered, a delphinium whose soaring elegance needs staking.

This is not the professional needing to impress his visitors, it's how gardeners who care about their gardens tend to behave. But it is hard for a professional not to have different standards from an amateur, if only because they are forced on him by other people. Alan came across this over the matter of a lawn mower. While talking to someone from a well-known firm of mower manufacturers he said casually that the box did not fit too well on his mower. Despite his protestations – he has no wish for special treatment – the rep was knocking on his door in a matter of days. They went out to the garage, the rep no doubt expecting a clean, burnished, well-oiled machine, put carefully away for the winter. What they found was the box bulging over with last year's mowings and the whole machine covered with a fine white film of dust, the result of mixing concrete nearby.

Alan is happy to admit to failure, even in the more sensitive matter of growing plants. To be defeated by *Dionysia aretioides* may not be too humiliating; it is classed as 'a difficult connoisseur's plant' and the alpine specialist Will Ingwersen refers to its 'undeniable intractability'. More surprisingly Alan says that he has never been very successful with carrots. It's not carrot fly – not many of the roots even reach a size where the fly would be tempted. It is hardly necessary to say that he's still trying, if only because he likes their fluffy tops.

But being a professional does affect his attitude to his garden. He admits to ambitions to grow things that other people can't, even crossing the delicate line between sensibly adapting to his conditions and rising to a challenge. He is also more aware of fashion in gardening than most amateurs. He does not share the popular belief that herbaceous borders are out – in knowledgeable circles they are in, especially if they are mixed with shrubs and roses – but rockeries, he says, are out. His own favourites tend to correspond with current fashions – old roses, irises, hellebores, snowdrops, hostas and annuals. He flies in the face of fashion by growing alpines in the two rock banks, but only those which survive without too much fuss and bother. He also has his dislikes – scarlet salvias, gladioli, French marigolds (though currently he is trying a new variety so that he can say from experience how revolting they are) and anything planted in rows.

He does not think of gardening as work, it is an absolute passion. 'My poor wife must get absolutely fed up with me. I read gardening books, I garden during the day, I organise seeds I'm going to plant in the evening. I really think I must be a tremendous bore.'

He is not. His 'great raw pleasure' in gardening is a wonderful thing to meet and a source of endless delight to him. 'There's no way, at half past eight in the evening, if the sun is shining, that I want to be inside in front of a television, when I could be sitting on the chamomile seat. It's just so nice to be among the fragrances and the colours. It's a heck of a lot of work, but I love it desperately. It's great.'

SHEILA
MACQUEEN

A FLOWER ARRANGER'S GARDEN

A SHOP window displaying a brown urn, a few leeks in flower and some old man's beard – these simple ingredients, shuffled by the imaginative hand of Constance Spry, ignited the seventeen-year-old Sheila Macqueen's love of flower arranging. 'Anybody who could make anything so pretty out of such rubbish knew something I wanted to learn.'

Fifty years ago Sheila, already dreaming of arranging flowers on Atlantic liners, had surprised her mother by the way she had done the flowers for her brother's twenty-first birthday party, so together they had gone to the only place that taught flower arranging at the time, the Sylvester School of Floristry. Sheila took one look at a conventional bride's bouquet – white carnations and asparagus fern, archly displayed on a music stand – and whispered to her mother that if that was what they were learning, then she wanted nothing to do with it. A few minutes later, walking down Bond Street, they passed Atkinson's perfumery shop and Sheila caught her first glimpse of the work of the as yet barely known Constance Spry.

Constance Spry, who was to be credited with 'bringing the country to the town' and who also had a great reputation as a hostess, introduced a more natural use of flowers in the house, arranging them as they grew and using a range of material that delighted the drawing rooms of pre-war London. When she combined red roses with purple cabbages in a marble bowl, the news even reached the ears of a startled porter at Covent Garden Market. Sheila began training with Constance Spry in 1932, just as interest in this new way with flowers and plant material was transforming the London floristry scene so fast that within two years the staff had increased from eight to seventy-six.

Socially Sheila's parents might have expected something different from their daughter, that she would be presented at Court, do 'the season', play tennis and

Beyond the peony-flowered double poppies, Sheila Macqueen's four-hundred-year-old cottage is covered by 'Lemon Pillar' and 'Constance Spry' roses.

go to parties. Indeed Sheila admits that her grandfather was quite horrified at the idea of her working in a shop. However, both her parents were artistic and loved flowers. Apart from the fact that she earned so little they virtually had to pay her to go to work, they were happy for her to do what she enjoyed.

And enjoy it she did. Soon she was taking lilies to the Duke of Windsor at Fort Belvedere, doing flowers for the Duke of Kent at St James's Palace, for Princess Elizabeth's wedding and the Coronation. Then Sheila started lecturing to Women's Institutes and in 1959 she went to Australia for six weeks to do the demonstrations for Constance Spry, who would never arrange flowers herself in front of other people, least of all a large audience. Sheila earned a little pin money, but mostly it was just fun and half the fun was that she didn't have to do it.

In 1960 all this changed. Her husband died suddenly and she was left with very little money, two teenage children to bring up and school fees to pay. Flower arranging, her great pleasure, now had to provide her with an income.

Over the last twenty-five years she has lectured, broadcast, taught and written several bestselling books, not only inheriting the mantle of Constance Spry (who died the same year as Mac, Sheila's husband) but becoming someone whose advice is sought by the flower arrangers of several continents.

There are those who teach flower arranging by rules – the correct size of vase in proportion to the flowers, the length to which different stems are to be cut, even spelling out which flowers are to be used and how. Sheila teaches as she works, instinctively, saying, 'It's basically something you do without quite knowing how you do it.' This refusal to rely on theory or rules is at the heart of her success as a communicator, though she finds that their absence makes teaching difficult. She teaches with her hands rather than her voice, pulling an arrangement apart to show what she means, removing one clear red rose from the centre of an arrangement to show how the mood changes, like seeing the smile disappear from a child's face.

When she began to give lectures she found that her audience, new to the whole subject of flower arranging, were interested in the most basic things. She might spend ten minutes explaining how to fix the wire netting in a vase to provide support for the stems. Now she finds that people know much more and prefer to watch her work. So surrounded by her equipment, in what one Australian admirer called a 'highly organised sludge', she may do as many as ten different arrangements in one lecture. There will be one for a table, one using a little cup in a candle-holder, a basket filled with treasures – in summer it might hold cyclamen, willow gentian, violas, daisies, heathers and a few heads of clematis. She may do a spare oriental arrangement, just three flowers in a shallow dish, or a great spectacular centrepiece. There may be one arrangement done to complement or blend with something in the room, for instance placing a trough underneath a picture and reflecting the colours. Sheila does not favour the flamboyant or the exotic, preferring a more realistic approach which relates the flowers to the rooms and their inhabitants. This practical approach has made her able to encourage and inspire a keen group of miners' wives in Nottinghamshire, whose enthusiasm was as great as their supply of material was small, as much as

Alabaster vase blending roses 'Fantan', 'Jocelyn', 'Amber Light' and 'Vesper'.

those lucky enough to have more abundant choice, like her audience at Winkfield, Constance Spry's school at Windsor, or at the Royal Horticultural Society's Garden at Wisley, where she still lectures two or three times a year.

In fact those who listen to Sheila Macqueen will find that despite her dislike of rules and theory, there are certain principles underlying her teaching – and the first one is the importance of looking at the room in which the flowers are going to be. (When she worked for Constance Spry they never did a vase of flowers without first going to look at the situation, whether it was a private house, a church, a cemetery or a banqueting hall; she once travelled from London to Brighton to see a small flat before doing just one vase of flowers.) She then decides on a colour theme, linking up pictures, furnishing, carpets, even ornaments, and only then decides on the position, the container and the sort of plant material she is going to use. The choice of container is less important where there is a plentiful supply of material, crucial if she only has three daffodils and some catkins.

Once she has picked or bought her flowers, her first concern is to get a good background; she prefers light, delicate material like tamarisk, cow parsley, grasses or ferns, the graceful outlines of *Abelia grandiflora* or the curious twists of *Corylus avellana* 'Contorta'. Then she decides on a focal point; this might be a peony, a rose or what she calls 'a flower with a face', like a hellebore, a pansy, a dahlia or an open rose. For a fan-shaped arrangement in an urn, she places the tallest stem, usually one and a half times the height of the vase, first, urging that it should be firm and straight or the whole arrangement will lean with it. She then places two shorter stems of different sizes, one on each side, then two more, again both shorter and of different length. A stem of almost the same height as the first is placed horizontally, giving the outlines of the fan shape. It says much for the work of people like Sheila that this approach is now virtually standard practice.

Mixed spring flowers in a pewter mug.

She insists that these are approximations, suggestions, not rules. It is because flower arranging is a creative highly personal art that so many people find it both relaxing and challenging. But when someone has raised flower arranging to such a peak as Sheila has, then amateurs do well to heed suggestions, however tentatively given: that to tuck large leaves at the base of the vase 'cleans up' the whole arrangement; that stems should not be shortened until they have been held in position – after all, you can't put the severed stem back on; that each flower should play its part and be seen as a whole flower, not overshadowed by another; that a colour can be encouraged to predominate by recessing it deep into the arrangement; that blocking flowers in colours avoids a spotty effect; that in choosing materials one should go for quality, not quantity.

On the choice of containers she likes the unusual rather than the gimmicky, a distinction none the worse for being ultimately personal. She has collected containers all her life and knows the value of a bright blue goblet, filled with delphiniums or gentians, a fragile china vase for primroses, an earthenware pot for dried grasses. She will treasure a vase that may only make a rare appearance, feeling that its brief life on show is worth keeping it long months on the shelf.

Given her enthusiastic reaction to Constance Spry's bowl of leek seeds and old man's beard, it is no surprise that Sheila's choice of material is not limited by the range available at the average florist's shop – anything, animate or inanimate, may appeal to her imagination. A fungus found on a country walk inspires an arrangement of iris, peonies, creamy honeysuckle and the fasciated stems of an evening primrose; the rough texture of a stone contrasts with the smooth leaves between which it is placed; courgettes, aubergine and apples surround the stems of an arrangement for an autumn party; a basket of vegetables and herbs decorates a table for a barbecue; a vine branch, some poppy seed heads, dock leaves, cow parsnip and honeysuckle, secured in a pin-holder on a plastic tray, provide an arrangement worthy of the most elegant setting.

Sheila has had flowers in her own house since she was first married and had so little furniture that she did huge arrangements to fill up the space. She will always have something, even if it is only a mid-winter moss garden in a soup plate with a couple of *Iris stylosa* (now known as *I. unguicularis*) and a few twigs. Flower arranging is something which she loves and needs and of which she never tires. Even though, as a professional, she feels she must not be caught out by the numerous keen gardeners and flower arrangers who visit her home, she could

A walled corner overhung by 'Golden Showers' and 'Maiden's Blush' roses. The raised bed in the double wall is ideal for tender plants.

The herbaceous border closely planted with delphiniums and *Campanula lactiflora*, with a 'New Dawn' rose in the foreground.

not, in any case, bear to live in a house without flowers. She loves to be able to enjoy the individual flowers as close as her hand, to show them to her friends without having to trail down the garden on a wet summer's evening, to walk through a room wafting of honeysuckle. She admits that on the telephone she is sometimes only half listening, distracted by wondering if an arrangement is quite right, whether a flower or piece of foliage needs moving or replacing.

Is Sheila first a flower arranger or a gardener? If pressed, she will say she is first a flower arranger, though to see her archetypal English garden, the cottage walls smothered with roses, clematis and winter jasmine, the sparkling health of her plants and their immaculate abundance, is to realise that the competition is close.

Her love of gardening began when, as a small child, she helped her grandmother prick out seedlings and learnt traditional garden lore. 'If you take a cutting, plant it near a stone, because it's cooler and helps the roots to get going.' However, she feels that no one is really a gardener until they have their own garden, so she would date her life as a practical gardener from soon after the war, when she and her husband settled down in Hertfordshire and began to develop the two and a half acres that she has tended for thirty years.

The Macqueens had lost their hearts to a pair of derelict cottages, four hundred years old, condemned and with no electricity, water or drainage. The two gardens, divided by iron bedsteads, were full of nettles and old tin cans. Were it not for a few vegetables, some fruit trees, a white cherry and a small walnut, it could not have been called a garden at all.

They loved it. Every free moment was devoted to developing it, at first systematically – Plan A, Plan B, Plan C – always with a picture in their minds of what the garden would one day become. First they cleared away the iron bedsteads and old tin cans, put down a lawn for the children and gave some geese the run of the grass and weeds. Then they started the first border, at right angles to the house as Sheila prefers to look along the length of a border rather than head on. Now this luxuriant border ribbons round, encircling the house, pausing for the small drive and giving way to shrubs before it disappears gently into a quiet woodland area, where foxgloves and bulbs thrive beneath the trees. There are more borders to the side of the house, a vegetable garden at the back, a small patio and a south-facing terrace with plants in tubs, in small groups and growing in the paving stones. A border of particular interest to flower arrangers is the spectacular gold border. Here she grows *Spiraea* 'Goldflame', two irises, *I. spuria* and *I. pseudoacorus* 'Variegata', whose leaves are striped with yellow in spring and excellent in flower arrangements, *Euphorbia griffithii* and *E. polychroma* and any gold hostas – she finds she can never have too many.

But to describe Sheila's garden is like trying to catch mercury. While her husband was alive he felt they had developed just about as much as they could manage. Twenty-five years after his death and with only a little paid help, Sheila still cannot resist changing, experimenting and developing new areas. She is painfully aware that it can only get harder to keep up as she gets older, knows all too well that one of the maddening things about gardening is that as you acquire the knowledge to do what you want, so you are less able, physically, to do it; but nothing stops her or keeps her from working long hours.

Although Sheila's garden has a gentle charm and a variety of interest that delight hundreds of people on her yearly open day and the countless groups, like the National Society of Decorative Arts, who come to visit it, the design of her garden is secondary to her need for a storehouse, an outdoor larder, from which she can cull the ingredients she needs for her arrangements.

Most of all she needs foliage. 'Grow the foliage,' she says, 'you can always buy the flowers.' So for what she calls 'leaf sculpture' she has broad leaved plants like bergenias, globe artichokes and hostas. There are leaves grown for their colour – lime green, which she finds the best colour for blending, blue, red, and such silver-leaved plants as she has left after a severe winter. Her collection of variegated leaves must rival that of any private garden in the country. She has variegated honesty, astrantia, phlox, sedum, weigela, holly, willow, solomon's seal, poplar, cornus, philadelphus and even variegated ground elder, which is not so invasive as the ordinary variety, but which has a perverse tendency to grow where she doesn't want it and not to grow where she does. For the feathery outlines she loves to give to her arrangements she grows thalictrum,

Hostas, one of the flower arranger's most useful plants.

grasses, lady's mantle and ferns – but not the over-used asparagus fern; angelica and poppies are there primarily for their seed heads and *Skimmia japonica,* several varieties of holly and cotoneaster for the berries. Her favourite flowers, the icing on the cake, include spring bulbs, geraniums, astrantia, aquilegia, lilies, delphiniums and lobelia to satisfy her love of blue, and her great love – roses. Of the flowering shrubs she grows viburnums, chimonanthus and witch hazels for winter colour and in spring she has azaleas, though as they are slow growers she picks them with caution.

Sheila has useful advice for anyone starting a garden with an eye to flower arranging. Grow at least some of her ten most useful plants – lady's mantle, artichoke, Italian arum, bergenia, euphorbia, ivy, hellebore, hosta, pokeberry and sedum. Five of these, once established, will provide the basis for a flower arrangement throughout the year. It comes as no surprise to notice that most of these are foliage plants.

With no theoretical training as a gardener, Sheila picked up what she knows simply by growing the plants she needs and wants and observing them closely. Three aspects of gardening have become particularly important to her – feeding, propagating and knowing the best varieties. It took her a long time to realise

how much plants benefit from feeding, that it is as important to spend money on fertilisers and mulches as on the plant itself. She is now a generous feeder, using fish, blood and bone, compost which she makes herself and spent hops, which she feels have been most helpful to her clay soil. In her early days as a gardener she was constantly short of money, buying plants in twos and threes or even singly, so she became skilled in propagation. She still grows many of her plants from seed or cuttings and the back of her house is like a small nursery as trays of seedlings and plants, even trees, in pots jostle for space, some destined for her own garden, many on sale to the public. She is constantly looking out for better varieties of plants, constantly persuading others to do so too. She prefers *Nepeta gigantea* to the more usual *N. faassenii*, the pale yellow *Achillea* 'Moonshine' to the strident 'Gold Plate'; she has some unusual hybrid peonies from the American specialist, Sylvia Saunders, a tree wisteria and several less usual roses – 'Constance Spry', 'Chianti', 'Tigoire', 'Madame Caroline Testout' and 'Chaucer' are among her favourites and she is especially fond of David Austin's roses 'Dame Prudence' and 'Charles Austin'. Sometimes she produces her own surprises, like two astrantias, which crossed accidentally, producing a splendid plant with short petals and flowers tinged with green, pink and white.

When it comes to picking her flowers Sheila has a problem. She grows flowers and foliage in order to cut them, then finds she has become a gardener, wanting to leave them where they are. Sometimes the decision is made for her. If visitors are coming round the garden, the flowers remain in the ground, if she is giving a lecture or making a television appearance and needs the flowers, then she cuts. But often she anguishes, sometimes dithering half a day over some special plant, like a lily. Should it crown an arrangement in the house or continue to complement the delphiniums, which, after all, it had been planted to do? There is, however, an art to picking, and Sheila has mastered it. She is always careful to pick without destroying the group she has so carefully planned. She keeps the shape of a shrub and finds she hardly has to prune after the shrub has flowered – she has pruned as she picked. There are always the flowers she grows especially for picking, like gladioli and dahlias, and in summer she can usually spare some roses.

Sheila the flower arranger and Sheila the gardener are, in practice, allies rather than rivals. She treats her garden like a vast arrangement, planning a patch of garden as she might a vase; she arranges her flowers to look as they might in the garden. She is a creative artist who uses plants just as surely as a painter is an artist who uses line, colour and texture – this is her great pleasure. But she gains an even deeper satisfaction when she communicates her enthusiasm to someone else. 'I do flower arranging because I love it and I want other people to love it. If there is just one person who comes up after a lecture and says, "I'm going straight home to do it myself", then the whole day has been worthwhile. It's a lovely feeling, feeling that you've inspired someone to want to arrange flowers themselves.'

The large decorative leaves of *Geranium psilostemon* surrounded by the pale yellow *Achillea* 'Moonshine', a standard wisteria, delphiniums, and *Alchemilla mollis*.

PROFESSOR
ALAN GEMMELL

THE SCIENTIFIC APPROACH

FOR a long time Professor Alan Gemmell considered himself a scientist, not a gardener. Over the years the balance has shifted. Now, retired – or perhaps it would be truer to say semi-retired – in the Isle of Arran, he is as captivated by the art of gardening as by the science.

The young Alan Gemmell was a reluctant gardener; he did not garden because he wanted to but because his parents told him to and he obeyed. Admiring, as he does, the Victorian virtues of discipline and self-control, he feels with hindsight that it was good for him, even though he objected at the time. He didn't even choose to read botany. He was already launched on a course in chemistry when his mother said, 'You're not a chemist any more, you're going to do a degree in botany.' So he did. This was not merely a maternal whim. It was 1930, the great depression was looming, jobs were hard to find. A neighbour had said that if Alan could get a good degree in botany, then he – at the time Head of the Plant Husbandry Department of the West of Scotland Agricultural College – would give him a job. So Alan Gemmell became a botanist.

He was a good botanist. A first class honours degree, a Commonwealth Fellowship, followed by an advanced degree in plant pathology and plant physiology at the University of Minnesota, laid the foundation for a distinguished career, leading from lectureships in Glasgow and Manchester Universities to his appointment in 1950 as Professor of Biology at Keele University. He has had a spell as a Home Office biologist, been visiting professor at the University of Shiraz, Iran; acted as biological adviser to the Universities of Malawi, Lesotho, Botswana and Swaziland, Sierra Leone and Cuttington College, Liberia. He has published articles on plant physiology,

The Gemmells at home on the Isle of Arran with Goat Fell in the background.

plant pathology, ecology, evolution and genetics in numerous scientific journals and his book *Developmental Plant Anatomy*, published in 1969, is still selling.

His time at the West of Scotland Agricultural College, where he conducted research in diseases of vegetables and food crops, led eventually to his becoming a household name in the world of amateur gardening, for in 1949 he was invited to join Bill Sowerbutts and Fred Loads on the BBC's programme *Gardeners' Question Time*. Originally cast as the team's scientist, he soon became equally valued for his summing up of sometimes differing advice and for his sense of humour. Ken Ford, the producer and chairman since 1962, writes of him, 'Once or twice we've had to stop recording when this sense of humour has got the better of him and he's collapsed into helpless giggles. One occasion was rather embarrassing as, with tears rolling down his face, he was unable to tell us what was so funny – it turned out to be the lady's hat in the front row.'

The famous trio stayed together for thirty-three years, always introduced by the familiar litany, 'Fred Loads of Burnley, Bill Sowerbutts of Ashton-under-Lyne, Professor Alan Gemmell of Keele University'. These credits originated in the principal of Keele's insistence that Keele should be acknowledged by name because, as a new university, it needed the publicity.

Although Alan Gemmell's familiarity with the physiology and diseases of plants enabled him to cope confidently with about half the questions they were asked, he was tentative at first, afraid to speak unless he was certain he knew the answer. But as he gave, so he received. He freely and gratefully admits that he learnt the craft of gardening not from a horticultural college, not through practical experience, but from his colleagues, Fred Loads and Bill Sowerbutts.

How then does a botanist, coming to gardening in middle age, view this new dimension to his professional life? He feels that there are numerous valid approaches. People garden for an income, for a source of food, as a recreation. For some the garden is primarily a place for their children to play, for others it is an art. While he finds most people's approach is too unscientific, he suspects that he undervalues the aesthetic.

'I don't look on plants as mysterious entities which for various reasons grow, I tend to look on plants as very attractive and beautiful machines, which if you oil the right way and point in the right direction, will in fact produce a result.' He regards gardening as an applied science, knowing that certain basic principles are almost universally applicable. 'You learn what different fertilisers do. If they do it to a cabbage, then they do it to a begonia or a palm tree.'

But there are exceptions, and this is where gardening differs from science. Alan Gemmell feels that trial and error, deduction and observation (and gardeners have to be good observers) can take you a very long way, but you cannot apply this sort of common sense without some basic horticultural knowledge. Why, for instance, should you plant a plum tree in the winter and rhododendrons in April or September? His answer is precise, if involved. 'Because evergreens such as rhododendrons usually shed their older leaves in spring, they do not suffer drought strains on the plant while the new leaves are very young, for new roots form very quickly. In areas where there are dry

A corner of dwarf conifers near the front door includes *Juniperis* 'Blue Star', *Chamaecyparis obtusa* 'Nana gracilis', and *Ch.* 'Plumosa', *Sequoiadendron* 'Adpressa' and a prostrate juniper, *Juniperis stricta*.

springs one should plant evergreens in September to allow root development before winter sets in. If you plant a plum tree in spring there could be a serious lack of water on tender foliage before its roots are established. But plums or other deciduous subjects can form roots very quickly in early winter or late autumn when the soil is still warm from the summer and so be ready for the new outburst of leaf formation and water loss in the spring and summer.'

Without some basic knowledge gardening looks like magic. Alan Gemmell, scientist to the fingertips, has no patience with what the professionals sometimes call 'muck and mysticism'. During his years on *Gardeners' Question Time* he saw his role as 'a voice crying in the wilderness of mysticism, of empirical knowledge, of traditional lore. I was saying, "Look, there is a scientific reason why things happen," and I was there to try to tell people what it was.' His fervour amounts almost to a sense of mission. 'I felt I had to take away the semi-mystical aura which has built up round gardening and which still exists today. It has now clothed itself in the pseudo-scientific jargon of environmental pollution and biological enemies and that sort of stuff, but a lot of it is still muck and mysticism under another guise.' He may have succeeded in changing the climate slightly, but there are still countless gardeners who say, for instance, 'the sap is rising' without having a very clear idea of what they mean. Alan Gemmell needs to qualify such a statement.

'I would have to say that water with contained substances is moving up the stems or trunk of the tree under a force which in general terms we call the transpiration stream, in order to provide materials for new growth. Since there are no leaves present to draw this material up, it must be pumped up from the base, but the exact mechanism of this pumping is not clearly understood. But I am quite certain that there is a mechanism which pumps liquid along in exactly the same way as there is what one might look on as a reverse mechanism which moves material down the tree in the autumn to be stored in roots and trunk. The phrase "the sap is rising" may be a shorthand way of saying this, but it is not an explanation, and should not stop experimentation to find out basic mechanisms which, once understood, may lead to better plant management.'

Alan Gemmell loves trying to explain scientific things to people with no scientific background and still does this, even now he is officially retired. He still writes regularly, his *Guardian* column is deservedly popular, he and his wife take parties round gardens all over England, Scotland and Wales, often as many as four a weekend; once a month he goes to Bridgemere, a small village in Cheshire which boasts the biggest garden centre in the country, to field questions from all comers; every year he deals with many more at the Chelsea Flower Show. He's also involved with writing software for computers. Gardeners with a home computer will soon be able to punch out a question asking, for instance, for a fragrant, yellow plant, five feet high, evergreen and tolerant of shade. Up will come the answer: *Mahonia japonica* or *M.* 'Charity'. Plans are afoot for a computer service to unravel the mysteries of plant diseases, so worried gardeners, beset by eel worm, club-root disease and coral spot, can receive advice twentieth-century style.

The Gemmells bought their cottage on Arran in 1968, for years only being able to go up there in the summer holidays. From the gardening point of view this was disastrous. They would arrive at the beginning of August to find the grass two or three feet high, the beds full of the most pernicious weeds. Alan even reached the stage of despair when he felt he would have to sell the place, it was just too much. Then, after a few weeks' hard work, everything at last under control, he would be off back to Keele again. It wasn't until 1977, when he retired from the university, that he was able to give the garden more attention. They moved permanently to Arran at the end of 1983.

He had, however, made a good start in the years when it could only be a holiday home. The cottage had been owned by a fisherman with more interest in the sea than in the land; it was, to put it bluntly, a mess. They had to clear away two and a half lorry-loads of scrap iron – old bedsteads, bicycle frames, wheels, tin cans – before they could begin to tackle the weeds, still less feed the undernourished soil. The only useful plants were a rhododendron which still blooms – he thinks it is 'Britannia' – and what seemed like acres and acres of rhubarb.

Alan Gemmell is keen to disabuse people of the idea that being so far north means it is very cold. The west coast of Scotland benefits from the Gulf Stream, so although it is about a fortnight later than the south, it is warmer than most southerners might expect. Visitors to Brodick Castle, admiring the palm trees and the banks of rhododendrons against a frequently clear blue sky, may have to revise their opinions. However his horticultural life is not without its problems – he enumerates four.

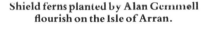
Shield ferns planted by Alan Gemmell flourish on the Isle of Arran.

The first is that, as the garden is on the side of a hill, the rock is very close to the surface, sometimes coming through the ground, so there are areas where the soil is very thin. The daffodils bear witness, some flourishing in a reasonable depth of soil, others half their normal height as they search in vain for nourishment. Secondly, soil conditions are made even harder by the debris from four old cottages, fallen down and still buried under the ground. Anyone used to more luxuriant conditions, confidently plunging a spade into the ground, could break a wrist. The third problem is the wind; being tucked into the side of the hill, they are more sheltered than their neighbours, but it can be very windy. Finally, the garden is north-facing.

Not, it would seem, the perfect site for a garden. But Alan Gemmell is undaunted. He does not like formal gardens and has no wish for a trim suburban plot, so it suits him very well. It is between half and two-thirds of an acre, on a gentle slope, mostly in front of the house and on each side of it; the back slopes steeply up the hill. There are now five island beds, a long shady border on the west side, several shrubs and small trees in the lawn, a wall for alpines, a bank of ferns, a narrow border running down the edge of the short drive and an interesting corner of evergreens near the front door. It is not a garden of great vistas and avenues – though the view across the bay to Goat Fell is enviable; Alan Gemmell does not aspire to a billiard table lawn, rather he calls it 'a botanical experience'; the soil is poor and he does not attempt to grow difficult plants. But it would be unwise to jump to conclusions. A friend of the Gemmells' came to take photographs of the garden, at first thought there was nothing to take and found himself spending two entranced days taking pictures. It is not an obvious garden, but the more you look, the more you find.

In his book *The Sunday Gardener*, Alan Gemmell writes that when you plan a garden, the first thing you must decide is its purpose. For him, as for most gardeners, the purpose is pleasure. What gives him the most pleasure? 'Oh dear, that is rather like asking whether you prefer champagne or caviar.' He is a tall, strongly built man, and his pleasure, fortunately, includes the physical work, even, to his own surprise, weeding. He enjoys the noticeable improvement and 'the fact that you can sing to yourself, talk to yourself, think your grandest thoughts and, because it's not demanding intellectually, I write a lot of my articles mentally while I am weeding.' He finds cutting the grass a soothing occupation; he enjoys, most of all, walking round the garden in the evening, rejoicing in what he has created, delighting in the view of the sea, the hills and the islands where he has chosen to create it.

He describes himself as a working gardener, who cuts every blade of grass himself and is proud of the dirty hands that are an inevitable part of gardening; as a scientist he is also an observant gardener, enjoying looking at plants closely, in very great detail. He is also a pragmatic gardener, accepting that plants will die without letting it distress him too much, even, as a scientist, experimenting with plants that are not likely to flourish in his conditions. Sometimes he fails – phormiums simply couldn't tolerate the incessant rain; sometimes he confounds the theorists by succeeding where, strictly speaking, he should not.

Conifers and ferns protected by a windbreak of native trees.

91

Alan Gemmell knows exactly what he wants from his garden. 'I don't mind if there are daisies in my lawn, I don't mind if there are weeds around. I am not going to devote my life to creating a perfect garden, because life is too full. I want to be able to play golf, I want to be able to write and to do umpteen other things. In order to make a perfect garden you have to be willing to devote your life to it. What I want is to be happy in my garden. It's a marvellous soother and easer of minds. There's a kind of timelessness and endlessness about a garden. The seasons change, you change the plants in the garden, but it's still there.'

It is in the plants, not the aesthetic appearance of the garden, that Alan Gemmell's satisfaction lies. He calls it 'a semi-plantsman's garden'. By this he means that he doesn't collect plants just because they are there, driven by a desire to have every variety of a given species, he collects the ones he enjoys. Anyone who gardens on chalk, or in areas where hard frosts are always a danger, will envy the range of plants he can take for granted – fuchsias, pittosporums, hydrangeas, rhododendrons. Unwilling vegetable gardeners will admire his resolute stance, despite the years devoted to food crops – 'I think vegetable gardening is for young enthusiastic people with big families.' He has a practical approach to the reality of advancing years and has some useful labour-saving ideas. A particularly effective one is the way he has planted the evergreens by the front door. He covered the area with dustbin liners, cut a cross where he wanted to plant, then fitted the polythene snugly up to the stem. A covering of stones from the beach and he has a virtually labour-free corner – all he has to do is clear away the leaves in the spring.

Alan Gemmell gardens in the full realisation that it will be here when he is not, agreeing with the old saying, 'You should look at your garden as if you were going to die tonight and plant it as if you were going to live for ever.' So what does he choose to grow? He likes plants that are 'not extraordinary, but a wee bit different'. So of the willow family he grows *Salix* 'Hippophaefolia', *S. alba* 'Britzensis' and 'Vitellina', *S. daphnoides, S. hastata* 'Wehrhahnii', *S. caprea*, the 'Goat Willow', and his most recent acquisition, 'Kuroyanagi'. Of the maples he has chosen *Acer ginnala*, for its spectacular autumn colour, *A. negundo*, also known as the 'Box Elder', *A. capillipes*, with its attractively striped bark, *A. palmatum* 'Dissectum Atropurpureum' and 'Heptalobum Osakazuki'. The scientist in him objects quite strongly to people having plants in their garden whose names they do not know, and it is important to him not only to know every plant by name, but to know its history, where it came from, how it has developed. His professional life leads to some acquisitions which makes the amateur's eyes rather greener than, perhaps, his fingers. For instance, he was once given seventy hebes (Hillier's *Manual of Trees and Shrubs* lists seventy-nine, so it was virtually a complete collection), in lieu of payment for a lecture. Unfortunately a very bad winter killed many of the more tender varieties, but he still has about thirty. Another day he was going round Windsor Great Park with the head gardener, when he saw an unfamiliar plant with bright, metallic blue pods hanging from it. It was the deciduous shrub *Decaisnea fargesii*. He asked for some pods, took them home, washed out the slimy mucilage, realising that it

**Mrs Gemmell's favourite viola,
'Jackanapes'.**

Primula pulverulenta **prefers a shady position.**

might contain an inhibitor to prevent the seeds germinating in the pods, put them in the fridge for three months and planted them. They germinated, survived and are growing well. He regards this as one of his greatest triumphs.

He has few dislikes. One is the enormous marsh-loving plant, gunnera, which he describes as 'rhubarb in barbed wire sauce', and despite his generally relaxed attitude he admits to being exasperated by the weeds – ground elder, creeping thistle, creeping dock, creeping buttercup, brambles, nettles – that blow remorselessly in from the neighbouring fields. But he does have his favourites. 'Garryarde Guinevere', one of the loveliest of the primulas, *Rodgersia aesculifolia,* with its leaves like giant's hands, *Ophiopogon* 'Nigrescens', the only black plant, which sits on the earth like a great spider and viola 'Jackanapes', a particular favourite of his wife's. He seldom grows annuals, preferring shrubs, and he has some winners – *Clethra alnifolia,* the sweet pepper bush, *Enkianthus chinensis,* an American shrub with spikes of cinnamon-scented flowers, the silver-leaved shrub *Euryops acraeus,* and the calico bush, *Kalmia latifolia,* which endears itself to him particularly because of its tenuous hold on life.

Despite his delight in plants for their own sake, Alan Gemmell shares Gertrude Jekyll's view that just as a collection of words is a dictionary, not a novel, so a collection of plants is not a garden. He aims at a pleasing association of plants, a blend of colour, texture and habit. Is this the artist coming out? The scientist in him still shudders at words like creative, personal, artistic, but he accepts that his attitude has changed. This dates from his first appreciation of the importance of touching living organisms – he feels you can learn much about someone simply by watching them handle plants. Now he can say that where gardening was for him mostly a science, now it is also an art. Old habits die hard, and he still tries to suppress the emerging artist, but to see him stand over a tiny, barely visible, shoot, enthusing over the joys to come, to hear him talk about Arran, is to know that he is not quite succeeding.

To him Arran is 'an inherited disease'. All the families there have either known the island for generations or will know it for generations and the Gemmell children's love of it was one reason for their decision to make it their home; now the Gemmells can share their grandchildren's delight. Alan can indulge his interest in wild flowers and enjoy the peace which he appreciates more every year. They can also, at last, see Arran all the year round, watching the changing colours and moods.

'In the winter the bracken is golden brown, the heather a darker brown, the twigs of the young birch are purple and, where there is still grass, it is greyish green. When spring comes everything changes to bright green as the new bracken emerges; on the beach there is bladder campion, sea lavender, sea aster and sea holly. It stays bright green for most of the summer, because it isn't usually dry for long – the sea sparkles and there are seals, porpoises and you can see the fins of basking sharks. People think the autumn is sad, but here it is very lovely because just as things are dying down, the heather comes out purple and blue, sometimes lit up by brilliant sunsets, and the hills over Kintyre are bright blue. There is a very slow change to winter and by mid-November you realise that the bracken is gone and it's all dark brown and purple again.'

Arran seems a good place for retirement, and gardening the ideal occupation. When the weather is good Alan Gemmell works in the garden or plays golf; on bad days he writes, when he couldn't garden anyway. He is a contented man.

PERCY
THROWER

BRITAIN'S HEAD GARDENER

WHEN Percy Thrower was a boy, soon after the first world war, the training ground for gardeners was private service. His father being head gardener of a huge estate in Buckinghamshire, he could hardly have had a more auspicious start. Percy's one ambition was to follow in his father's footsteps – perhaps, one day, he too might be a head gardener?

Horwood House was owned by an Irish bacon millionaire. It totalled nearly 500 acres, of which about fifteen acres of fields and woodlands had been developed by Percy's father into an impressive garden. To be in charge of such a place, to be head gardener, was to be one of a small select group, respected by the community, feared by the men who worked for him. Mr Thrower and his staff of nineteen grew a wide range of plants on a scale which makes most of today's private gardens appear Lilliputian. The avenue of lime trees was a quarter of a mile long, the rock garden covered an acre and a half, the kitchen garden, enclosed by walls ten feet high, was over two acres. There was an orchard with a fine collection of 200 fruit trees – two dozen varieties of apples alone; the greenhouses were skilfully used to ensure fresh fruit and vegetables all the year round and provide the flowering plants and cut blooms needed for the house.

Percy began to work full-time for his father when he was fourteen. It was a tough life for a young boy. He started at six thirty in the morning, did an hour and a half's work before breakfast and went through until five thirty. Even then he was not finished, tools had to be cleaned, oiled and put neatly away in his own time. His first job was in the greenhouses, sweeping floors, crocking pots, cleaning out the stoke hole. Soon he progressed to pricking out seedlings and potting up young plants. He was rewarded with a shilling a day, earning the odd extra sixpence for trapping a mole, shooting a magpie or opening the gates for the huntsmen. Sometimes the meticulous, short tempered Mr Thrower would throw his cap across the greenhouse at any unfortunate lad whose work was short of perfection – Percy was once at the receiving end of his father's cap for accidentally breaking the stem of a calceolaria.

Percy's early training is something quite unavailable today. This is not just

Adding peat to the Shropshire soil enables magnolias and azaleas to flourish.

96

The PH of the soil was originally 6.5. Adding peat has brought it down to 5.0, enabling this nineteen-year-old *Azalea mollis* 'Exbury' hybrid to flourish magnificently.

because the standards are less rigorous, but because methods have changed, making many jobs easier and quicker. For instance, most gardeners in the 1980s, both professional and amateur, assume they will use a ready-mixed compost like John Innes. In those days mixing the compost was a skill to be learnt, each head gardener having his favourite recipe for different groups of plants. At Horwood they would leave stacked turves and manure for a year to form the basis. It would then be pulled to pieces by hand and the appropriate additions made. It might be leaf mould, or silver sand from Leighton Buzzard; a little brick or coal dust would be added for cyclamen, small bones for chrysanthemums. Slow and cumbersome though it must have been, no one who has spent so long humouring a plant so carefully is likely to forget its tastes and preferences.

Percy must have shown promise, for after four years, when his father felt his son should get more experience, he astonished him by suggesting he went to the Royal Gardens at Windsor. He wrote to the head gardener, C. H. Cook, and soon Percy found himself at one of the top gardens in the country, earning a pound a week.

At Windsor Percy was one of sixty gardeners, working in a disciplined hierarchy as strict as a ship's company. Directly under the head gardener, who patrolled the gardens dressed in black jacket, pinstripe trousers and bowler hat, were five foremen. Each foreman was responsible for one department, each allocated his own tools, equipment and compost, and woe betide anyone who borrowed a spade and failed to return it promptly. Three specialist growers looked after the orchids, the chrysanthemums and the carnations. These nine men were the élite, the officers, holding responsible well paid jobs and rarely

Magnolia soulangiana. The Throwers named their house 'The Magnolias' at the suggestion of *Amateur Gardening* readers.

moving on from Windsor. Humbler tasks, like stopping and thinning vines or tying back after pruning, were done by journeymen gardeners assisted by improvers. So precise was the distinction between the ranks that whereas improvers were each given a knife, the accolade of a budding knife was only awarded to a journeyman.

Percy was one of about twenty young improvers, all living together in a bothy, reputed to be the finest in the country – they were even provided with a billiard room and a wireless. He spent his first two years in the fruit department, under a former colleague of his father's, Mr Waltham. Growing fruit under glass is a highly specialised art and it would be hard to find anywhere better to acquire the necessary skills. The fruit houses of Windsor stretched over a mile, a quarter of a mile for each of the four seasons of the year. They grew cucumbers, melons, strawberries, figs, apricots, plums, peaches, nectarines, cherries, grapes. Meeting royal demands meant strawberries must be ripe for Easter, grapes, peaches and nectarines had to be on the table on May 26th, for Queen Mary's birthday. The standards were almost ludicrously high. One cracked vine shoot, one finger mark on a peach and the force of Mr Waltham's not inconsiderable personality was let loose on the offender. Percy met this over the matter of a peach tree. Tying in the branches of a fan-trained peach was a job that could take a whole day. Percy's first painstaking efforts were rewarded with a long critical look and three words, 'That won't do.' Mr Waltham silently took a knife and, tie by tie, he undid the whole day's work.

It was just as well the improvers had each other's company in the bothy, for working at Windsor must have been a frightening experience, especially as they knew that any lapse, any drop in standards, could mean the sack. In those days to leave a job without references was to have little hope of finding a comparable job again. They were constantly supervised. At first everything Percy did, watering, top dressing, ventilating the greenhouses, was done under Mr Waltham's eagle eye. Later, as he began to work alone, it had to be done exactly as he had been instructed or a reprimand was inevitable.

Much of the fruit was pot-grown, a practice Percy continues in his own garden to this day. He remembers potting endless plants, using the wooden rammers that were obligatory at Windsor. Mr Waltham would be in and out of the greenhouse, watch in hand, timing how many strawberries were being

Water lilies surrounded by *Primula bulleyana* and *P. beesiana* hybrids, *Mimulus* 'Royal Red', and the golden yew, *Taxus baccata* 'Aurea'.

potted in an hour. At intervals he would pick a pot up and press the soil to see if it was rock firm. If his huge thumb left the slightest impression the pot was upended and the unfortunate culprit was made to start again.

After two years in the fruit houses, Percy was promoted to journeyman and moved to the plant houses. Here his responsibilities included filling the growing houses with plants for decoration throughout the year – cinerarias, salpiglossis, hydrangeas, pelargoniums, cyclamen, primulas of all sorts. He had to provide bedding plants for the terraces round the Castle, roses for the royal pavilion at Ascot and always he had to bear in mind the tastes of his royal employers. Queen Mary preferred pastel shades of pink, pale blue and silver; King George had to have a gardenia on the table at breakfast time every morning of the year. Percy's time at Windsor was to leave a permanent mark on his taste. His passion for fuchsias began in one of the long corridors off the show house, which housed a magnificent display of standard fuchsias. To this day he prefers the colours of the bedding plants he used to grow for Queen Mary.

Many of the young gardeners at Windsor were ambitious and long evenings at the bothy were spent discussing their prospects. What was the next rung on the ladder? Where, indeed, did that ladder lead? Always they came to the same conclusion – the future no longer lay in the private estates, costs were rising, promotion prospects were rare, indeed staff were being reduced. (By the end of the 'thirties Percy's father had had his staff reduced from nineteen to three.) The future, now, was in the public parks. So at the end of the summer of 1935, Percy left Windsor and took a job with the City of Leeds Parks Department.

At first he hated it. He was disgusted by the habit, then prevalent in parks gardening, of destroying bulbs and plants rather than caring for them during the winter and letting them bloom again. He felt limited by the emphasis on mass production and planting in serried ranks, he resented the time spent tending lawns and sports grounds. But he adjusted and when, after two years, he felt the need for a change, he joined another parks department at Derby.

Here he worked under a man he considers the finest head gardener he has ever known, John Maxfield. 'He was the typical old-type head gardener; he would look a man up and down and sideways to see what he was like and to ascertain if he was going to be any use to him. He judged a man in the greenhouse by the way he handled a watering can. Did he fill the pot right to the rim? Did he tap it to see if it really needed watering, or was he watering just for the sake of watering? If he had a man who used a can correctly he would do anything for him . . . He was very strict, very severe; but he taught me the heck of a lot.'

The war years saw many changes in Percy's life. One was that he got married. While he was at Windsor he had met Connie, the daughter of the head gardener, C. H. Cook. (Improvers were not expected to talk to the daughters of head gardeners, let alone court them, so this friendship alone ensured that Percy made his mark at Windsor.) They had arranged the wedding for the second Saturday in September, 1939. The declaration of war left them in turmoil. Should they go ahead with their plans or not? They did – in style. Mr Cook was by then head gardener at Sandringham and the reception, with over a hundred guests, was

An impeccable onion bed, 'Kelsae' and 'Robinson's Improved Mammoth'.

held at his house in the grounds. Percy's job changed too. He was put in charge of food production, using every corner of the land owned by Derby Parks Department to such effect that, though he volunteered twice, he was on both occasions told to carry on with his current job, as his contribution to the war effort lay in the job he was doing.

After the war Percy moved to be Parks Superintendent of Shrewsbury, which he quickly retrieved from a combination of neglect and the dictates of wartime economics. His first real challenge was what to do with the two-hundred-year-old lime avenue. The trees, at over a hundred feet, were too tall; worse, they were dangerous and a young girl had recently been killed by a falling branch. Opinions were divided as to what should be done. Some advised felling, some felt that topping should be sufficient. It was Percy who risked the displeasure of the people of Shrewsbury by insisting that they should be cut down. It took five years to replant, but he has never doubted that he made the right decision. Nor, when they saw the new young trees, better spaced and growing well, did his former critics.

There was pressure to use the greenhouses mainly for producing food, as fuel restrictions were still in operation, but Percy was not to be stopped from growing flowers. He cut begonia tubers into pieces, quadrupling the stock; he found fifty rather elderly fuchsias and, by skilful propagation, turned them into 5,000 in his first season. Fuchsias are still a feature of Shrewsbury, hardy and tender, as hedging or standards, in tubs, in borders, in hanging baskets. Also in that first year Percy became involved in a scheme to expand the two-day Shrewsbury Flower Festival into a summer-long display. Hotels, business premises, public buildings, even traffic islands, were bedecked with flower arrangements. Shrewsbury was beginning to deserve the title it was to acquire, the Town of Flowers.

It was while he was at Shrewsbury that Percy started broadcasting. On the first occasion he was interviewed with the two judges (one of them his father-in-law, C. H. Cook), during the Shrewsbury Flower Show. Soon after that a walk round the Dingle prompted an admiring Godfrey Basely to invite the man responsible to take part in a BBC programme, *Beyond the Back Door*. The success of the first talk – on making a small shrubbery – led to a monthly spot on seasonal work in the garden. It was done from the studio where, to the surprise of the technical staff, Percy insisted on defying convention and standing at the microphone rather than sitting. He then began broadcasting a series of programmes from other people's gardens. It was known as *Beyond the Back Door* until the owner of a small stately home protested. Perhaps stately homes do not have back doors? It became *In Your Garden* for the rest of its highly successful run. Television followed. Soon he was a regular contributor to *Gardening Club*, which became *Gardeners' World*, when television burst into colour and gardening programmes were given better placings.

After the first occasion, before which he was too nervous to eat, Percy enjoyed broadcasting, found it easy and appeared on numerous programmes, including *Woman's Hour* and the children's programme, *Blue Peter*. He soon

A cool combination of *Hydrangea paniculata* and japanese anemones.

acquired a massive following, becoming known as 'Britain's Head Gardener'; one would have thought he could have dictated his own terms. But the BBC thought otherwise. In 1976 he accepted an invitation to advertise gardening products on Independent Television and the BBC would not tolerate it. He was dropped. The popular press had a field day. 'Britain's head gardener Percy Thrower has been pruned by the BBC.' 'Top television gardener given the order of the Big Welly Boot by the BBC.' 'Percy Thrower finds himself in the fertiliser.' It was the BBC, not Percy, who were the losers. Percy simply transferred his attention to Independent Broadcasting and gave more time to writing. With hindsight he can take his place amongst those who forced the BBC to realise that it did not own its contributors.

The basic principles of gardening have not changed since the first tree grew in the Garden of Eden, but methods have in the last twenty-five years undergone a small revolution. Percy Thrower has lived through these changes, being forced to accept things that gardeners like his father and Mr Cook would have found quite shocking. For instance, at Windsor no one would have considered growing a plant in anything other than a clay flower pot. Now there are plastic pots, peat pots, whalehide and polythene containers. There are ready-mixed composts, packed in every size you could want, fungicides, pesticides, insecticides. The old methods are side-stepped, sometimes no longer even possible. Watering, for instance. 'I was given a cotton reel on the end of a cane and I had to tap a pot before I watered it. If there was a clear ring, it was an indication that it needed watering. If it was a dull sound, then it didn't. You could do that with a clay pot, you can't with a plastic one. Now you have to go by the weight, the feel.' Percy Thrower has had to change with the times and admits that, despite a lowering of standards which must distress anyone trained as strictly as he was, there are plants he can grow better with the new methods; he instances poinsettias and cyclamen.

The greatest single change has been the introduction in the 1950s of container-grown plants, a change which led directly to the start of garden centres. The amateur gardener especially likes to see the plant in leaf and in flower, to be able to ask advice about soil and position, then to take it home and plant it straight away. 'Instead of the till only ringing between November and March, it rang throughout the twelve months of the year. People could see money in it.' Percy saw money in it too, he is a good business man. In any case he was looking around for something he could do when he retired as Parks Superintendent of Shrewsbury.

In 1967 he was asked by ICI whether he considered Syon Park could be turned into a national garden centre. He did, and joined the board, taking such a large part in the development of the centre that at the opening ceremony he shared a car with the Chairman of ICI and the Queen Mother.

However, he began to find that he did not always agree with the way it was being run, feeling that the management was top heavy, that business could be more prosperous. More and more, he was seeing the potential in garden centres and when he heard that the long-established nursery firm, Murrell's of Shrewsbury, was for sale, he realised that this was a chance he must not miss. So Murrell's of Shrewsbury became Percy Thrower's Gardening Centre – a place that also offers tea and light refreshments and encourages people to 'Come and walk round in pleasant surroundings.' He realised that even if people bought nothing on one visit, they would, if they had enjoyed themselves, come again. Murrell's extensive catalogue was expanded, garden furniture, tools and general sundries were added, but more and more the emphasis came to be on container-grown plants.

At the garden centre they buy in plants they can't grow themselves, like the acid-loving azaleas, rhododendrons and camellias, but they grow huge quantities of stock in their own nurseries. About 100,000 shrubs and climbers are grown from cuttings every year, 7,000 cyclamen, 1,200 poinsettias, 1,500

A fruiting lemon, grown from a cutting, which crops heavily and enhances a gin and tonic.

calceolarias, 1,500 cinerarias and of course Percy's favourite, fuchsias – last year they grew 20,000. Percy admits that he doesn't always enjoy seeing a plant on which so much loving care has been lavished go across the counter for money, but he doesn't allow himself to be sentimental. 'You go into business to make money.' With 16,000,000 private gardens in the country and more than £1000,000,000 spent on them every year, there is plenty of money to be made by garden centres.

Percy was fifty before he was in a position to do what most real gardeners long to do – make his own garden to his own design. He has always been keen on shooting and in 1956 he and a friend bought sixteen acres of rough land, partly to shoot over, partly as an investment. One day, as the guns were being reloaded and lined up, he was standing looking at the view over the Wrekin and Wenlock Edge, the Stiperstones and Caer Caradoc, one of the most beautiful views in England. As he gazed, the thought came into his mind, 'What a place to build a house.'

The Throwers were living in a tied house at the time, so Connie and his three daughters did not take much persuading that this was a good idea. They obtained planning permission – a great deal easier in those days – fenced in an acre and a half of land and over a couple of years, built a house on the top of the hill and began designing a garden round it. At last he had a piece of land that was his own, that he could lay out and make himself. He expected it would take eight years to reach its full potential, though, such was his enthusiasm, he completed the basic work in just under four. Now, over twenty years later, he has a garden of which even he, with his rigorous training and exacting standards, is rightly proud and which he has no wish to change.

For anyone carving a new garden out of rough land, the first concern is to define its limits, to choose some form of fencing. Percy decided on hawthorn hedges, now reaching seven or eight feet, for the east and north boundaries, a retaining wall of local red sandstone for the side bordering the road at the bottom of the hill, with beech hedges inside the roadside wall and separating the vegetable garden and greenhouse area. The lawns, except for the areas nearest the house, were made by cutting the field grass regularly, eliminating weeds and encouraging the finer grasses.

He wanted an informal garden, a place that was beautiful, relaxing and blending naturally with its surroundings. He had plenty of space, he was fermenting with ideas. Where did he start? He was aware that he would not always want to do a great deal of hard physical work, so the first things he planted were trees. There is a handsome tulip tree, *Liriodendron tulipifera*, many varieties of *Prunus*, including 'Cheal's Weeping', 'Shirofugen', *P. subhirtella* 'Autumnalis', and two 'Amanogawa'; there is a golden weeping willow, a weeping birch, *Metasequoia glyptostroboides, Ginkgo biloba*, a group of cypresses, a eucalyptus, a cedar of Lebanon and a walnut tree. These trees provide a framework; sometimes they stand alone as specimen trees, sometimes shrubs cluster round them in informal beds. By judicious planting Percy Thrower has succeeded in his ambition of designing a garden which harmonises with the surrounding countryside. He has even managed to improve the stupendous view with which nature provided him. Now the garden slopes gently away between the house and the hills, a sea of green with islands of plants. By adding peat he is able to grow azaleas, rhododendrons, camellias, heathers and of course, magnolias. (Following the suggestion of his readers in *Amateur Gardening*, he called his house The Magnolias, so he could hardly be without them.) There are hardy fuchsias and hardy border plants; roses – hybrid tea, floribunda and old-fashioned; berberis, buddleia, viburnum and cotoneaster. He is tempted to grow things he knows are not really suited to his exposed situation and to his delight he has succeeded with two particular favourites, *Embothrium lanceolatum* and *Eucryphia nymansensis*, which is now over ten feet tall and flowers profusely for the whole of August.

One of the most attractive features in this garden, a rock and water garden, was constructed while the house was still being built. Two concrete rock pools are joined by a waterfall, the water being circulated by an electric pump; the surrounding stones are planted with rock plants and spring bulbs, the charming miniature ones like the hoop petticoat daffodil, *Narcissus bulbocodium*, angels' tears, *N. triandrus albus*, species crocuses and *Iris danfordiae* and *I. reticulata*. It took him a while to establish gentians, but after four or five attempts in different parts of the rock garden, he has been successful with *Gentiana acaulis* and *G. sino-ornata*.

He has planted drifts of the larger daffodils, with snowdrops, muscari, scillas and ornithogalum, along the drive and in the field grass. As they multiply he digs out the small new bulbs and plants them in a corner of the vegetable garden until they have reached flowering size. After a lifetime of gardening he still enjoys these jobs. Gardening is his hobby as well as his living and he never tires of it, except for what he calls 'fiddly jobs'. He hates spraying and admits that he doesn't do what he exhorts others to do – he doesn't read the instructions.

On the other hand, fiddly jobs in the greenhouse such as sowing seeds, taking cuttings, pricking out seedlings, training plants – these are jobs he happily does for hours, even after a long day at the garden centre. He has two magnificent greenhouses and several cold frames. He loves to have fresh fruit and vegetables and grows tomatoes, melons and cucumbers, as well as strawberries and potatoes in pots. One greenhouse is devoted entirely to strawberries, ready to eat by Easter, just as they were at Windsor. There are also fuchsias, geraniums, chrysanthemums, hippeastrums and orchids. There is more produce in the vegetable plot and the orchard – almost everything a cook could want is there, grown with the text-book perfection which is Percy's hallmark.

Every inch of Percy Thrower's garden is immaculate, loved and tended. Even the tools are kept so clean and tidy that they could be mistaken for new – he has not forgotten the strict training he received at Horwood House and Windsor. But the way the Throwers have decorated the area round the house deserves special mention. On the terrace there are tubs and troughs, in the spring full of bulbs, wallflowers and polyanthus, followed by fuchsias, geraniums, trailing lobelias and petunias for summer; on the north wall there are camellias and on the south there is a lean-to glass-house where Connie Thrower grows a fruiting lemon among her husband's fuchsias. It produces at least thirty lemons a year and Percy is convinced that it makes an unbeatable gin and tonic. Also on the south wall is a pergola, the poles planted in drainpipes sunk into the ground, so they can be easily replaced when they rot. Over the pergola Percy grows roses – 'Madame Alfred Carrière' and the thornless pink 'Zéphirine Drouhin', clematis, honeysuckle, passion flower and wisteria. More climbing plants adorn the walls of the house.

The Magnolias has become widely known through the television programmes that are made there, so perhaps the Throwers should not have been as surprised as they were when they first opened their garden to the public and 5000 people turned up. It gives Percy a great sense of achievement to see people enjoying his garden. It also has its humorous moments. On one occasion a local farmer called Tom Griffiths, who used to help tidy the garden before the public arrived, brought his wife to see round it. After a few moments he rushed up to Percy to tell him there was a weed in the rockery. They went to inspect and there, sure enough, was a seedling dock. 'Nay, Tom, that's no weed,' said Percy. 'If that isn't a weed I'll eat my bloody hat,' replied the outraged Tom. After everybody had gone Percy looked up the botanical name for dock, wrote a label *Rumex griffithi* and put it in the ground by the dock. By June it had flowers like a rhubarb plant. Nobody questioned it, not even Tom.

There is a wax model of Percy Thrower at Madame Tussaud's, he has been awarded the MBE, he has earned the sobriquet 'Britain's Head Gardener'. But he doesn't feel he has changed. 'I never look on myself as a celebrity. People say, "Oh, you're a celebrity", but I'm a gardener. I set out to be a gardener and I'm still a gardener.'

MARY SPILLER

A COTTAGE GARDEN IN THE TOWN

WE all have our own fantasy of a cottage garden. It enfolds, comforts, nourishes, heals. There will be honeysuckle round the porch, a gnarled old apple tree, old-fashioned roses, hollyhocks, lavender, columbine, poppies, lupins, sweet peas and herbs. The thought brings wafts of childhood and sunfilled carefree days, fragrant scents and the murmur of bees. Whether we have actually known a cottage garden or not, it calls up memories of perpetual peace and happiness. It has the quality of a dream.

For Mary Spiller it is a reality. But her garden does not lie quietly in some idyllic hamlet, it is not tucked away in a fold of some sleeping valley. It is on a busy road opposite a garage in the outskirts of Oxford, a few hundred yards from the British Leyland works in Cowley.

The house in which she now lives is one of two built at the turn of the century by her grandfather. His daughter, Mary's mother, was a sickly child and he was advised to move out of Oxford into the country. In those days Cowley was mostly farmland and the Spillers' house was surrounded by hayfields. Now the garden, which Mary has known all her life, is a tiny oasis in a desert of concrete – a long narrow garden, fifty yards long and five yards wide. When her grandfather died and the house was sold, Mary's parents kept part of his garden, so it widens out at the bottom. Later they bought an additional strip, so it now totals about a seventh of an acre.

As a child Mary had a little piece of garden that, in theory, she could call her own. In practice, every time she planted something in it, the adult world moved in, deciding it was needed for something else. It's a wonder she was not discouraged for life. In fact her first gardening memory is of boredom. Her father was Secretary of the Ashmolean Society, a natural history society, and she

A few hundred yards from the British Leyland works in Cowley.

still has a photograph of herself as an unwilling nine-year-old being dragged round Wisley Gardens in the pouring rain.

However, when she left school, knowing only that she did not want to be a nurse or a secretary, and that she did want an outdoor life, she found, almost without consciously deciding it, that she was training to be a gardener. It was during the war and she had intended to join the Land Army, but her father dissuaded her and she signed up for a course at Waterperry, the nursery garden and training centre near Wheatley that had been started in 1932 by the indomitable Beatrix Havergal and that, over the years, had acquired a world-wide reputation for training professional gardeners.

Waterperry was to become the pivot of Mary Spiller's horticultural life, most of her professional activities stemming from it. First, however, she needed qualifications and experience. The qualification she obtained was the diploma from the Royal Horticultural Society; the experience was practical. Together with a friend, she put an advertisement in *The Lady* offering their services. The responses varied from one woman who asked, 'Are you men, women or rogues?' to several offers of jobs which took them round the country, both advising on the development of new and run down gardens and actually

Left, a scented honeysuckle, *Lonicera japonica* 'Halliana', and beyond a 'Crimson Conquest' rose clothes the arch leading to the garden; *right,* a moss rose planted by Mary Spiller's grandfather over a century ago.

carrying out the work. Though she modestly insists on calling this 'jobbing gardening' it was in fact much more than that, as several gardens, notably one on Shotover Hill where she worked for many years, bear witness. Helping amateurs look after their gardens involves a whole range of sensitivities that are not needed when designing a big professional garden. Mary's insistence on understanding what people want from their gardens, in trying to please them, rather than simply impose a garden on them, was part of her success during this period of her life. She was not ambitious, she just found it great fun, but it soon became clear that she had a gift both for garden design and for growing plants. Her casual pursuit of gardening had become an addiction.

In the late 'fifties Mary Spiller started giving evening lectures for amateurs in Oxford and, as her reputation as a teacher grew, Miss Havergal invited her to lecture on flower gardening at Waterperry. Gradually this expanded to include classes for the Women's Institutes and in 1970, when Miss Havergal retired, Mary Spiller took over the training section completely. She is now one of the co-managers, though Waterperry is not a hierarchical place and people tend to drift into jobs rather than be appointed to them.

The job Mary drifted into includes a good deal of administration which she

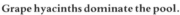

Grape hyacinths dominate the pool.

Crocus tomasinianus and snowdrops.

enjoys least, but it is unavoidable with eighty-three acres and a staff of about twenty-five. She does not have much to do with the selling, which is perhaps just as well for business, as her love of plants compels her to dissuade people from buying them if she doesn't feel they are going to be given the right conditions. Her real love is running the ornamental gardens, both building on Miss Havergal's basic work and developing new areas; she has made several new shrub and heather beds, she has extended the river walk and hopes to make an informal water garden. She also enjoys teaching. Waterperry ceased to be a residential college when Miss Havergal retired, but the courses, both amateur and professional, are as popular as ever.

It might be assumed that teaching future professionals is more taxing than teaching amateurs, but Mary Spiller feels that the reverse is true. Amateurs have probably been gardening for some time, they are for the most part older and will all know about different things, they ask more varied and awkward questions. (It is surprising to realise that many specialists are amateurs and many plants have been developed entirely by amateurs. Once they have taken up a subject they often learn a great deal about it.) On the other hand a group of young students, being fairly uniform in age and knowledge, presents different problems. 'It's more hard slog teaching future professionals because you've got to make them understand, you've got to make them remember, you've got to be sure that you've got everything done. But it is exciting when they pass their exams. I find teaching amateurs is more fun because their careers are not depending on it. You get much more give and take and many more challenging questions. You really have got to have your wits about you.'

A mass of foliage leads to the wild garden.

Mary Spiller is an outstanding teacher, knowledgeable, clear, imaginative and endlessly patient. It is no surprise that her classes are packed. It is no surprise either that when someone from Waterperry was needed to appear on television, it should have been Mary who was chosen.

It was in 1981, when they decided to open the gardens more often to the public to help pay for their upkeep, that *Gardeners' World* was approached. Perhaps they would like to do a programme from Waterperry? The producer agreed and Geoffrey Smith came down to introduce it. Mary's contribution, and a 'trial run' on building a raised bed for alpines, led to her becoming the first woman to be a regular presenter. It is sad that the whims of television are such that she is not, at present, to be seen on the programme.

At Waterperry everything has to be done properly. Almost all the grounds are open to the public, many plants are for sale and the highest standards are kept. So Mary Spiller wants her private garden to be just that – private. It is for her a pleasure, a place where she can relax, a place where she can, with impunity, let her high standards drop. 'It gets very much second-class citizen treatment, my garden.' She wants it to look nice, but it is not intended to look good simply for the sake of looking good. Still less is it meant to impress; if it were she would spend more time on the tiny front garden on the busy main road. As it is, the delights are in the back garden hidden from public view. Even there, charming though it is, she doesn't attempt to have an immaculate garden. She hates spraying, so she doesn't spray; she knows it needs a good dose of manure, but somehow she doesn't quite get around to it; she does not grow difficult plants and if a plant doesn't flourish – well, it gives up and dies. She does not cherish it and coax it back to life as she would at Waterperry. She is not prepared to be a martyr to her garden. 'If I want to go out but there's something that needs doing in the garden, I shall still go out, because I feel that I mustn't tie myself completely to gardening.'

So her garden is run on that understanding. It is a cottage garden that she wants to look good with the minimum of worry, though she is more precise and calls it a 'cottage-type garden' because it has a small lawn. Her aim is everyone's dream, but it takes a good gardener to approach its realisation. Mary Spiller's success must be seen in the context of these aims.

Books on garden design often advise us that we will see the garden most frequently from the sitting room (or the kitchen, or the bedroom) and that we should plan it to look its best from these vantage points. Mary Spiller is more instinctive, direct, courageous. An air raid shelter built during the war, blocking a window which has never been unblocked, means that none of her main downstairs rooms looks out on to the garden; in any case she knows very well what she wants from her garden and she has the knowledge and the confidence to achieve it. 'My garden is orientated round me in it,' she says firmly.

She loves scents, so she grows sweet briar, rosemary, thyme, lavender; true to the cottage-garden ideal, she has a scented honeysuckle romping round the arch which leads into the main garden at the back of the house. She likes to have water, so at various times she has had three or four different pools, changing them as the mood takes her. The current one is full of double kingcups, a particular favourite as they were given to her by a friend who is now dead; the surrounding small rock garden has one of the few rare plants in the garden, *Tropaeolum polyphyllum*, a perennial climber of the nasturtium family. The sites of previous pools are turned to good use; one is now a bog garden, providing a good home for the summer snowflake, *Leucojum*.

Much though Mary loves her pools, she is not prepared to walk round them on her daily journeys to and from the car at the end of the garden. She must have a straight path to the garage, but having made one she found it looked too much like tramlines running into the distance. Her love of graceful shapes would not tolerate this, so she solved the problem by putting down slabs of rough concrete as stepping stones across the lawn and sowing grass on the ash path. Now, with occasional mowing, it looks as she intended it should, like a little woodland path.

She grows few vegetables because they are so demanding of time, ('I sow broad beans and the blackfly get them, peas and the mice get them') though she says she will be more prepared to give them attention when she has retired. But she enjoys eating fruit, so she grows rhubarb, gooseberries, strawberries, raspberries, red currants, black currants, plums, apples and blackberries – a very good selected one with huge fruit, put in by her grandfather some seventy years ago. She is virtually self-sufficient in fruit, with enough of some crops to give away. Recently her neighbours took out a hedge and built a new dividing wall, so now she can grow apples and pears as cordons and espaliers. She is of course an expert on fruit growing, as her book on the subject testifies.

**The pool in early summer with a
magnificent white deutzia beyond the
lawn.**

Some weeds are allowed into this garden, some are hard to keep out. Rosebay willow herb makes a handsome show, horsetail makes a good mulch.

High on her list of priorities is the sun. Her passion for it is such that she has designed a garden full of little niches, each catching the sun at different times of the day. There is a breakfast spot on the lawn, sheltered from the north wind by fencing panels covered with clematis, winter jasmine and roses; to catch the evening sun she has nibbled an arbour out of the climbers which cover a wall at the bottom of the garden; logs lie around to act as a back-rest, a cup stand or a typewriter table. So if she is not actually gardening, she reads, writes, or prepares her Waterperry classes outside. Even a shaft of wintery sunlight will tempt her out. Most people want their gardens for pleasure, but not everyone is able to enjoy it; they are too busy worrying about how it looks, whether they have done everything they should, at the right time, in the right way. Mary Spiller practises what she preaches.

Despite her determination that her garden will not rule her life, Mary Spiller's garden has something flowering in it almost all the year round; in peak times it is a riot of colour. Let her take us through the year.

'In January the first flowers are usually crocus – very early ones like *C. lavigatus* followed in February by *C. tomasinianus* and the snowdrops, which go on till March. Then the hellebores, I would never be without them, double daffodils and all the spring bulbs following on. Next come the tulips, summer snowflakes, wallflowers at the top of the garden, aubrietia, grape hyacinth and lily-of-the-valley. Then as the tulips go, the border poppies and the aquilegias will be coming on; the aquilegias seed so profusely I just pull out the colours I don't like so much. As we get towards summer there are the hardy geraniums and the shining cranesbill – the wild geranium with its tiny, bright pink flowers which seeds everywhere and makes a wonderful ground cover. I've got a few lilies underneath the apple tree and there are phloxes, white bachelor's button and yellow loosestrife. I mustn't forget the shrubs – after the forsythia and flowering currant there are the kerrias – both single and double, genista and berberis, then potentillas and a rather nice white deutzia. The potentillas provide wonderful colour, they go on all through the summer really. Then I've got a few shrub roses and my grandfather's moss rose, it must be about a hundred years old now. I have a few bush roses because my mother likes a cut rose very much, but I don't think I'd bother with them for myself. Then there are the peonies, first the common red one, followed by the big named varieties; and *Euphorbia robbiae*, I love that, it goes on for so long. Midsummer brings the irises and philadelphus but August is a bit dull, because I'm usually on holiday in Scotland. Then in September there are sedums, Michaelmas daisies and golden rod – the right one, not the horrid one. I don't put in dahlias or chrysanthemums, they're too much work, so that really takes us to the end of the season, though there's still a bit of colour from the leaves and the apples. November and December are my barest months, I've got to work on those, but there are always the sempervivums – they're marvellous, the way they look so neat and colourful all the year round.'

Mary Spiller's garden adjoins neighbours on each side, as any town garden does, but the luxuriant dense planting provides some privacy and gives the

A weed with a story, Oxford ragwort.

enclosed protected feeling that she wants. There is a framework of trees and large shrubs – a *Chamaecyparis lawsoniana* 'Ellwoodii', *Berberis stenophylla, Rhus typhina, Philadelphus* 'Virginal', holly, lilac, the huge blackberry and the confusion of climbers where the birds nest. There were some elms, which succumbed to Dutch elm disease, and a willow, which grew so large that she had it lopped back to a stump; such is the resilience of willows that already it is shooting up again. Recently she has planted a mountain ash which she had been given. She feels it is probably too big for her garden, but she was keen to have one, because of the tradition that a mountain ash keeps the witches away. The question was, where to plant it? The traditions conflicted – one saying it should be planted on the north side of a house, if it is to be effective in keeping off witches, another that it should be near the door. Mary chose the latter, though being uncertain *which* door, she chose the back door. After all she uses it more often, so perhaps, given the chance, the witches would too?

Mary Spiller has divided her garden loosely into the part near the house, which she calls the cottage garden, and the further end, the wild garden. Here there are elderflower, ivy, blackthorn, primroses, bluebells and cowslips. The

Enchanter's nightshade enjoyed by a leaf-cutting bee.

Euphorbia robbiae, a special favourite.

first cowslip arrived by happy chance in some turf; she saved the seed and later generations supplied both her own garden and Waterperry. She also encourages her inheritance with packets of wild flower seeds. Recently she has sown cuckoo flower, moon daisies and balsam.

She is keen to encourage wild life in all its diversity, at least as much diversity as living in central Cowley permits. If this attitude permits plants, even weeds, that would make the owner of a trim suburban plot shudder, she is quite unperturbed. In fact there is a sense in which she puts animal, bird and insect life before the plants. Nettles are allowed limited ground space for the benefit of the butterflies; holes in the ground where bumble bees are making their homes are left carefully undisturbed; ivy, polygonum, forsythia, virginia creeper and hop grow in glorious abandon over a huge building in the next-door garden, providing nesting sites for the birds; the enchanter's nightshade, which even Mary admits is a tiresome weed, is left for the delectation of the leaf-cutting bee, who enjoys removing little half-circle morsels from it. Her care is appreciated. Urban encroachment has inevitably discouraged wild life; there are no longer newts in the pool and the nightingales were driven away some years ago, but there are still hedgehogs, foxes and rabbits (though they prove a bit much even for such a keen nature lover), frogs, dragonflies and butterflies; and a veritable conference of birds – blackbirds, thrushes, robins, sparrows of course, spotted fly-catchers, tits, both great and blue; swifts fly overhead, though she cannot persuade them to nest, black-headed gulls find it a pleasant place to visit in winter.

It is sometimes hard to understand the horror with which many gardeners greet anything which might have the misfortune to qualify as a weed – which, after all, is just a plant growing in the wrong place. But Mary Spiller has many reasons for allowing a limited number of non-invasive weeds in her garden.

There are not only the needs of the wild life to consider, with her wide-ranging love of nature (her hobbies are watching deer, badgers and birds) Mary quite simply likes weeds. She wants to paint a picture with plants, and as long as she gets the effect she wants, she does not mind if technically they are classed as weeds. She is particularly fond of, for instance, the Oxford ragwort, partly because, if one stops thinking with labels, it is quite a pretty plant, but also because it has a history. It was brought to the Oxford Botanic Gardens, from where it escaped by seeding on to the walls, first of the Gardens, then of the colleges. Soon it was being carried around the countryside by the trains and seeding along embankments. Now it is universal.

There are other weeds to which she gives a qualified welcome, many of them coming originally from the hedgerow that used to divide the two gardens and from the wild field, now a tennis court, that stretched away at the bottom of the garden when she was a child. It has left its legacy of cow parsley, bryony, and Jack-in-the-hedge, another name for hedge garlic. She fights a losing battle against the horsetail that sprouts out of the lawn, but makes the best of a bad situation by using the tops as a mulching material. The knock-down argument for anyone still unconverted to the value of a few weeds in their garden is that Mary Spiller has a professional interest in them. She has recently been writing a book on weeds and how to control them and there were some, like white dead nettle, which she longed to pull out, but had to leave in order to run trials on the numerous weed-killers on the market. Like any conscientious writer she is not going to recommend, or indeed condemn, products whose advantages and shortcomings she does not know from experience. She is still waiting to see whether the weeds she has treated will have the temerity to appear again next year.

Mary Spiller has no need to test her professional skills in the privacy of her own home – they are abundantly proved in places like the herbaceous border at Waterperry. She says that it is not the expertise of gardening that she is keen on now, it is the results. But it takes expertise and the confidence of the expert, to know what you want and to achieve it.

Oriental poppies Mary Spiller was given by a friend from Avebury. So she calls them 'Avebury Crimson'.

JOHN BROOKES

GARDENING BY DESIGN

'MISTAKES committed in this art are too important to be tolerated, being most exposed to view and in a great measure irreparable, as it often requires the space of a century to redress the blunders of an hour.' The writer was the architect, Sir William Chambers, the date 1772, the subject – garden design.

Every time a gardener chooses a plant, every time he decides where to plant it, he is venturing into this highly complex art, where not only are mistakes hard to redeem – and become harder with the passing years – but where materials are constantly changing: flowers come and go, leaves change colour and drop, plants, for the most part, become larger, bushier, more numerous. More often than not the amateur gardener meets this challenge alone, at best with the written word to guide him, yet advice can be sought from garden designers. One who is in demand all over the world is John Brookes.

Art and horticulture, the two skills involved in John Brookes' chosen work, both, in different ways, derive from his family. At school he excelled in drawing, a talent he inherited from various artistic relations. His interest in gardening began less positively. As a rather lonely small boy he was offered sixpence for every bucket of weeds he removed from his father's garden. This he did, not so much for financial reward as in an attempt to earn the love of a difficult father with whom he did not get on.

His father was a passionate vegetable gardener and despite the poor relationship between them (perhaps still trying to please him?) when John had left school and done his military service, he set off to study horticulture, which by then he enjoyed. He went to the Durham School of Agriculture, in the event finding commercial horticulture appealed to him so little that after a year, when he was offered a scholarship at Reading University, he tried to persuade the authorities to let him change to the landscape course. They refused to change the scholarship, he refused to continue in horticulture, so, there being at the time no other university course in landscape design, he went to Nottingham Parks Department on a three-year apprenticeship.

A bold use of architectural plants. Foxgloves surrounded by phormiums, and *Cordyline australis*, with *Hedera canariensis* 'Gloire de Marengo' clothing the wall.

The students spent six months in each of the sections. He liked the first five, soft wood propagation, hard wood propagation, working in the walled vegetable garden, setting out bedding plants and flower cultivation, well enough. He enjoyed working with plants and he did his share on the back of a tractor, but for John the high point of his time at Nottingham was the last six months which he spent in the design office. At last he was doing what he wanted to do. At the end of the course he sent some of his drawings to the former student of Gertrude Jekyll and pioneer landscape designer, Brenda Colvin. She gave him a job doing everything from making the tea to doing tracings of garden plans; at the same time he did a part-time course in landscape design at University College, London, which gave him a diploma. When Miss Colvin moved to Gloucestershire, he became assistant to Dame Sylvia Crowe, with whom Miss Colvin had shared her office.

It was 1960, an exciting period in landscape design. 1951 had been the year of the Festival of Britain, when the influence of modern design from the continent began to cross the Channel and Russell Page, Peter Shepherd, Frank Clark, Maria Shepherd and Peter Youngman had created the Festival Gardens on the South Bank. The 'sixties were about to swing in, bursting with a crazy creativity which was to affect design in gardens as it did in dress. Sylvia Crowe was at the peak of her distinguished career, the doyenne of current landscape thinking and at the time President of the Institute of Landscape Architects. John worked with her on many large-scale commercial projects, designing gardens for new towns, power stations and civic centres, and was able to see her designs realised and blossoming.

Wide ranging though Sylvia Crowe's talents were and much though John admired her, like any creative person he began to yearn to work on his own. He was realistic enough to know that he was not likely, so early in his career, to make a living by relying solely on private work, so, to the surprise of his friends, though with the support – for which he has always been grateful – of the designer/architect Geoffrey Jellicoe, he joined the magazine *Architectural Design* as an editorial assistant. The job kept him busy all afternoon and often into the evening, but left him with the mornings free to start his own practice.

It also gave him time to develop his own ideas on garden design. He admired the way Sylvia Crowe was 'doing it from the heart, with feeling and sensitivity, blazing a new landscape trail'. But by then he had begun to lecture himself, first at the Institute of Park Administration, then at the Royal Botanic Gardens at Kew, he was also writing for magazines and having to deal with the ensuing correspondence. More and more he found he needed a theory to back up his practical experience and his instinct.

John Brookes is concerned first with people and what they want from their gardens, secondly with the relationship of the garden to the environment, thirdly with creating a framework, a structure, for the garden and lastly with plants – he feels that most people go wrong by thinking only of the plants.

He sees landscape design as an art form and every person's garden as an expression of the people living in it. It is the relationship of people to their gardens that stimulates him – the creation of an outside room that will harmonise with the house, enhance their lives. Every aspect of living is incorporated into his designs. It is not just a question of lawns, borders, terraces and beautiful specimen trees, but of accommodating dustbins, oil storage tanks and garages, providing a sandpit for the young children, space for cricket and football as they get older, room for vegetables, a swimming pool, a greenhouse – anything that goes into that area that we loosely call a garden. He is essentially a contemporary designer, who would like to be remembered as someone who consciously related the garden to the current mood of society. He is also very aware that, even though they want it looking well, people are not necessarily prepared to spend a lot of time working in their gardens, there are too many other activities competing for their attention. So designing a garden that is compatible with the effort the owner is prepared to put into it is high on his priorities.

The border at Clock House. *Hebe andersonii* **'Variegata',** *Cordyline australis,* *Trachycarpus fortunei, Robinia pseudoacacia* **'Frisia' and** *Buddleia davidii.*

He stresses the importance of seeing the garden in the context of its environment – it is not an isolated piece of land, but a part of it. What is beyond the site is almost as important as what is inside it. So the boundaries of a garden are given great attention. Is there a view to which he wants to draw the eye? Or does he need to conceal an eyesore or draw attention from it? He likes to let the garden blend with its surroundings, rather than seeing it stop suddenly as it gives way to fields, woods or the neighbouring house or garden. He would not, for instance, plant a eucalyptus, which comes from Australia, on the perimeter of a garden which adjoins a very English beech wood. He would rather use garden forms of the local wild plants, muffling the border; he is keen to learn to manage wildness and might have an area of wild garden on the boundary, with the added advantage of cutting down on maintenance.

His next concern is the bones of the design. Basic design rules are the same,

Euphorbia characias, fig and *Phormium tenax* **'Purpureum' as a foreground to a wall covered with** *Solanum jasminoides* **'Album' and** *Ceanothus* **'Cascade'.**

whether it is a beautiful Georgian coffee pot, the fine lines of an aeroplane or a well-cut suit of clothes; it is simply that some are working in silver, metal or cloth while he uses gravel, grass, water and plants. He likes to see a garden in winter, preferably when it is covered in snow and there is absolutely no colour to distract the eye. Then he can see the pure shape, the masses and voids. He challenges his readers to look afresh at landscape in his most recent book, *A Place in the Country*. 'Look then at the shapes created by field patterns. See how the local hills or downs roll and unfold, note the placing of trees in a valley bottom, and the way they thin out as they grow up the hill, observe the flow of water – the run of a fast stream compared to the gentle meander of a brook on chalky levels. Experience the enclosed feeling of being between hedges or totally enveloped in a wood, and then emerging into open fields. Moving from enclosure into shade and then into light, you will be conscious of form. It is to the form of a landscape, or of a garden, that one instinctively reacts, feeling that the place is an interesting one, or on the contrary that it is . . . just unsatisfactory.' A garden for John should be a living landscape, a sculptured composition which you are in rather than on, where the spaces are as important as the masses.

An undogmatic approach is the key to his relationships with clients as a working designer. He has no interest in creating a garden independent of a site or a person; adamant that good design is conditioned by usership. Clients who say, 'Oh Mr Brookes, you give us what you think, you know best,' infuriate him and he has no patience with designers who are 'putting up little memorials to themselves, paying no attention to what surrounds it or how people are going to use it'. So only when he understands his clients' wishes and needs, when he is familiar with what is outside the garden as well as the area of land itself, does he get down to the drawing board. How does he create a garden that blends with its surroundings? How does he relate the garden to the house, the two flowing together so that house and garden are a harmonious unit?

Eventually he came up with a theory which he still teaches. A garden can be anything from a six-foot square back yard to several rolling acres, it still involves scale and interpretation. Whatever the size of the project he is tackling, John will start by drawing a detailed plan. First he will do a scale drawing of the outline of the house, measuring and marking the windows, doors and any strong features or jutting corners, then the garden, its boundaries, allowing for overlapping foliage, permanent structures like a garage, a mature tree, steps, internal walls and fences. Next he lays tracing paper over this ground plan, marking lines at 90° to the house or the boundaries, using strong features as reference points. Then, taking the same distances which separate these lines, he will mark another set at 90° to the first set, so the paper is covered with squares. The grid, which at this stage will look hard and geometric, provides a basic pattern on which he can allocate areas for specific functions – a terrace, a border, a water garden or an area for vegetables. He can design these in any shape he pleases, using curves, circles, squares, rectangles or abstract shapes; he can plan a garden which is formal or informal, traditional or modern, static or dynamic. By working in this way, a method which owes much to architecture, anything he designs will have a pleasing balance and harmony which it would be difficult to achieve by eye alone.

So far the plan is two dimensional, with masses to indicate where the planting will be. Now the third dimension, height, is added, as the difficult but exciting decisions are made – what to plant where. The garden is becoming a living thing.

It is the part that gardeners most enjoy, but it is bewildering. The choice is endless, the considerations daunting. John Brookes imposes order on what could be chaos by organising thought, identifying hazards. His logical approach gives a firm foundation to individual creativity.

There are many factors which must be taken into consideration before settling down with the catalogues. Is the garden in the town or the country? What is the soil type? Is it a windy site and is a screening of dense trees and shrubs necessary? Are there hard frosts? Areas of shade require special care, but need never be dull; there are numerous plants that not only tolerate shade but demand it. Is the air polluted? This modern hazard can endanger or at least inhibit some plants. Would it be wise to provide some protection against noise?

Then he groups the plants themselves and their special purposes. They can give shelter, supply food, provide sweet smells, please the eye. There are plants primarily for foliage, from the feathery lightness of artemisia to the shining plates of rodgersia leaves, shading from translucent green to deep red. There are plants especially useful for their form – John loves the sculpted shapes of hostas, verbascum, acanthus, yucca. There are plants for colour – landscape designers are not, as some people tend to think, indifferent to colour, but they do insist on using it well. John likes to plant in ranges of colour and is mindful of the natural colour cycle, starting with white and yellow in spring, intensifying through blues and reds, flaring into gold and russet in the autumn and returning to brown and grey in the winter. Weighing up these considerations not only clarifies the mind and confirms what one really wants, it imposes some limitation, which in a field of almost infinite choice, is helpful.

When he has reached the stage of composing beds, John will consider working on site, putting in stakes for trees and visualising the final result, but he prefers to continue planning on paper. His ultimate aim – and every garden designer has to think several years ahead – is a luxuriant, overflowing border, the plants spilling through each other, contrasting and blending in colour, form and texture. He also tries to ensure that it will have at least shape, and preferably colour, throughout the year.

He insists that just as the garden has been designed in proportion to the house, so the plants must be in scale with the garden. Their eventual size, how they are grouped, how many of each plant is used, is vital. He prefers bold groupings to single specimens, as 'a strong garden plan will always be weakened by the liquorice allsorts effect caused by the one-of-this-and-one-of-that type of planting.' He has support from nature herself, for plants rarely grow singly when left to themselves. Odd numbers are more dynamic than even numbers and for an average sized garden he recommends groupings in threes or fives. But the key is scale, it cannot be dogmatic.

Verbascum olympicum **backed by** *Catalpa bignonioides* **'Aurea', with the golden hop** *Humulus lupulus* **'Aurea' smothering the wall.**

He plans the planting logically, dividing the plants loosely into six rough and frequently overlapping categories. First there are the individual plants, the 'specials' or 'prima donnas' as he calls them. This might be a specimen tree, it might be an architectural plant like yucca or acanthus; it will be the focal point, the plant that determines the character of the bed. Then he adds the framework against which the plants will be seen – evergreens and climbers to contain the area and ground-cover plants that set off the other plants rather as a carpet sets off furniture. There is then a context to receive the decorative shrubs and herbaceous perennials, which need to be chosen for colour contrast and harmony, shape, texture and flowering times. Splashes of colour can be added by including bulbs and, particularly in the early years, annuals.

While choosing inside these categories is made easier, it involves detailed knowledge of plants and their habits and is, in the end, highly personal. In any case, plants come and go, and for John that is half the fun. He encourages people to include their favourites, to extend their knowledge by visiting other gardens, reading books, consulting catalogues (he favours Nottcutts, who list plants in colours, size and height especially for the designer and the student), but once the selection has been made, 'You must then be ruthless and eliminate about half the number you have selected, and double up on the remainder. The most common mistake of the inexperienced is to plant too much.'

Over the last fifteen years John has put his theory of garden design into practice in a variety of ways. He has elaborated it in numerous articles and bestselling books; he has seen his designs win medals at the Chelsea Flower Show. He has yet another outlet in teaching – he has taught design for many years at the Inchbald School of Garden Design in London and in Iran, where he took the opportunity to research for a book he is writing on the gardens of Islam. Now he has his own school of garden design in Sussex, a Mecca for students from all over the world – youngsters from garden centres, women hoping for a career when their children have left home, older men looking for a change of job. He takes people through his methods, helping them to produce a working plan and then interpret it in their own way. By doing this he has seen that other people can use his principles, whether in this country, Australia or South Africa.

The happy situation in which he now lives and works had its origins in 1973, when he took a group of students round Denmans, a garden near Arundel created by one of the unsung heroines of garden design, Joyce Robinson. He was immediately struck by the affinity between his work and her bold exuberant plantings, her love of architectural plants, above all her use of gravel. He was himself using gravel for London gardens, finding tiny muddy bits of lawn were pointless. Here he found the same technique used in a country setting, gravel and grass interweaving as ground cover, with huge groups of plants springing from it, the gravel carried to the feet of the plants, so paths merge with borders and no earth is visible. He loved its contemporary effect and the apparently natural profusion that conceals a strong structure and skilful management. He was convinced that this was a technique from which garden designers could learn.

Phormium tenax **'Purpureum' softened by** *Artemesia arborescens*, **with beds of African marigolds and feverfew kept in check by a gravel path.**

'The great secret is to allow everything to ramble and seed itself broadly; the only labour is to thin out what is not needed, rather than to plant what is. Thus, after the initial cultivation of the ground, into which the bones of the garden are planted, the only continuing cultivation is the late autumnal application of well-rotted cow dung between the plant masses. There is also, of course, a certain amount of cutting out and thinning down.'

He was also attracted to an old stable block in Mrs Robinson's grounds, collapsing and used for storage. Would she let him buy it? She would not, people were always asking her that, she replied. However, he persisted and at last they came to an arrangement. She was in her eighties and suffering from rheumatism, her children were not interested in taking over the garden and her devoted gardener, Bertie Reed, was retiring at the end of 1984. He could have the stable block on a long lease and when Mr Reed retired he could take over the running of the garden. It suits them both admirably. While there is breath in her body Mrs Robinson is not going to relinquish completely her control over thirty-five years work, or give up gliding round the garden in her electric buggy, but now she is secure in the knowledge that it is in the hands of someone who knows what he is doing and whose tastes so perfectly accord with her own. John has a home, a base for his school of garden design and three acres of garden to manage and develop.

The stable block, now called Clock House, has half an acre of land that is his own, where he can enjoy gardening as a hobby, where he can please himself. Had his father allowed it, he would have gone to art school when he was younger; he is more an artist than a gardener, more a designer than a plantsman. 'I'm not your down-to-earth horticulturist. I don't give a damn about pest and diseases, most plants are easy enough to grow anyway. I love line, pattern, shape and form. I love putting plants together to make compositions.'

His own garden is, as he commends for others, 'a room outside'; house and garden flowing together with the harmonious inevitability that comes only from careful planning. He has achieved this sense of unity by carrying through themes from one to the other. Container-grown plants are used both inside and outside; flooring and walls are carefully chosen and matched. The dining area gives on to a patio, the table placed near the glass doors, so whether winter or summer, there is no sense of division. The illusion that house and garden are one is heightened by a pergola, shading the area immediately outside the house, giving it intimacy and privacy. Just beyond there is a strong, well designed garden table, half hidden by plants and an alternative eating place when the weather permits. House and garden are for relaxing, living, sharing.

Beyond the patio John has treated his half acre in two related but distinct ways, to the right a large area of lawn stretches over to Mrs Robinson's garden and to the South Downs beyond, at right angles to the house there is a spectacular border.

It is above all a generous garden, generous in its planting, generous in its relationship to the adjoining land – Mrs Robinson's three acres. Where many people would have put up some sort of screening or fencing to ensure privacy,

John has been more subtle. The drive forms a boundary between the two gardens, but there is no vertical division and both he and Mrs Robinson profit from its absence as the two gardens merge and blend, each private, yet pleasurably aware of the other. The sweeping area of lawn is planted in big groups, similar to Mrs Robinson's, though in lawn rather than gravel. John has strong views over the shapes of beds. 'I hate island beds – an island bed is just a plonk. I can't bear them in any form – boomerangs, sausages, harpoons or pear shapes.' He favours what he calls 'floating beds', in this case one end is attached to the drive, the rest drifts gently round in a big S shape. This bed, planted with bamboos, fuchsias, hostas and cotoneasters, gives protection enough, but allows him to glimpse the garden beyond. By obeying his own mandate, that style should be, above all, in sympathy with its location, he is both giver and receiver. In opening out his garden he is also letting the outside flow in.

Having ensured that the garden blends with its environment, John was free to express himself in a more personal way. The great south-facing wall that runs the length of the garden is a perfect place for his special plants. Here he has planted a mediterranean cypress, the late-flowering *Catalpa bignonioides*, the white form of *Buddleia davidii*, the Mexican orange blossom, *Choisya ternata*, *Aralia spinosa*, known as the Devil's walking stick because of its viciously spiny stems, *Eucalyptus gunnii* and several varieties of cistus and coloured sages. There are also many of his favourite architectural plants – verbascums, euphorbias, cordylines, yuccas, phormiums, acanthus and cardoons, the strong shapes softened by wisteria, golden hop, clematis and ivy. Despite John's protestation that he is not 'a down-to-earth gardener' his plants grow so profusely that little ground cover is necessary, but there is the bright blue *Ceanothus thyrsiflorus repens* and in spring a carpet of bulbs. Though he does not put colour first, there is plenty of it, with wallflowers, geraniums and petunias used discreetly and perennials like anthemis, helichrysum and *Kniphofia caulescens*, with its soft coral red flowers, great stems and beautiful grey leaves, which John prefers to its more common relation the red hot poker. This wall provides a hot sheltered situation and he is able to grow subjects that would succumb to frost in many areas, like *Pittosporum tobira*, which is much used in Southern Europe for hedging, and *Mimosa dealbata*.

There is one drawback to John's enjoyment of his garden – it is not completely private, both his garden and Mrs Robinson's are open to the public. Further, as he runs his school of garden design from the house, there are often students around. He is publicly practising what he preaches, open to criticism as to praise, and is inhibited from experimenting as he might if he had complete privacy. Perhaps he would not change it very much, but his feelings about it would be subtly different – he would be freer. He has, in any case, the conflicting feeling that many gardeners have about their own gardens. On the one hand he feels content with it the way it is, on the other, he admits that half the joy of gardening is planning what to do next year.

A London garden designed by John Brookes.

131

DR STEFAN
BUCZACKI

A BOTANIST IN HIS GARDEN

NARCISSUS fire, witches' brooms, smuts, gummosis of cucumber, chocolate spot, bitter pit, anthracnose of willow – the names may sound romantic, droll or incomprehensible, but for most gardeners they represent a phalanx of the enemy. Stefan Buczacki, however, faces the army of plant diseases with fascination rather than dread, for though he is something of a polymath, he is above all a plant pathologist.

As a child he wanted to be a naturalist, first and foremost a zoologist. He had a huge collection of animals, including some exotic snakes and lizards, but the school did not encourage living specimens into the classroom, only allowing pupils on the zoology course to see animals pickled in bottles. So he switched his allegiance to botany, going on to obtain a first at Southampton University, with geology as second subject. In his final year he specialised in plant taxonomy and mycology, the study of fungi.

In childhood a keen stamp collector, by nature someone who likes things in categories and pigeon holes, he enjoyed classifying, naming, studying the evolution of plants and their relation to each other. His choice of mycology was, in the first instance, more hard-headed. He did not feel that the purely academic study of taxonomy was likely to get him a job, whereas the applied science of plant disease might. It did, and in 1971 he started work at the National Vegetable Research Station in Warwickshire.

For thirteen years he was a member of the Plant Pathology Department, one of eight research leaders, each with a small group of assistants, working on different aspects of vegetable disease. What motivates a plant pathologist? For most, it is the interaction between two organisms, the fungi trying to get the better of the plant – an unequal struggle, usually leading to the devastation of the victim. For Stefan the fascination lies even more in the organism that is doing the damage and its role in the contest. So much so that he sides rather more with the fungi than with the plant under attack. For any plant pathologist the object is to try to understand the pathogen that is causing the damage, then to learn to control it, but, unlike the human pathologist, he does not have to be concerned

Steps leading to the sunken terrace which Stefan Buczacki was delighted to restore and plant.

132

for the victim – the plant is expendable. When Stefan was working on club-root disease his research caused the death of some tens of thousands of cabbage plants; his primary aim being to further knowledge about the organism, this did not worry him. There is no place for devotion to individual plants in the laboratory – there cannot be.

An inheritance of mature fruit trees.

Though he enjoyed the work, indeed the purpose of his university studies had been that he should have a career in research, and though he soon achieved an international reputation in his field, after a few years disillusion began to creep in. He had great respect for the team working for him, but he became increasingly disenchanted with the senior levels of management in the agricultural research service, finding it hard to come to terms with the bureaucracy of a government institution. His personality began to change, he was even accused of being a loner, which greatly surprised people who knew him in private life. 'Actually doing research, designing experiments to the best of my ability, getting results, interpreting them, publishing them, did give me, and continue to give me, enormous satisfaction. But I began to withdraw into myself and set my own research goals and objectives.' He also began to divert his considerable energies into developing outside interests. He is ambitious and very able, feeling 'you only come this way once, so you might as well make the most of the opportunities you have been given.' So there was plenty of scope. He has always been a compulsive writer and, finding he had a talent for communication, he started a regular yearly course in plant pathology at Warwick University which he still runs, began writing articles for the popular gardening press and embarked on the definitive book on garden pests and diseases in collaboration with Keith Harris, an entomologist from the Natural History Museum in London.

Stefan first acquired a taste for broadcasting when he was still an undergraduate, through taking part in *Treble Chance*, a general knowledge quiz between universities, but his gifts behind the microphone had to simmer on the back burner for several years while he pursued his career in research. Eventually,

A member of the onion family, *Allium ostrowskianum*.

as visions of a freelance life became increasingly attractive, his thoughts returned to broadcasting. He had been interviewed by local radio about a book he had written on mushrooms and toadstools and on impulse he sent a copy of the tape to Ken Ford, the producer of *Gardeners' Question Time*. He was in luck. Not only did Ken Ford feel he had a good broadcasting voice, but Alan Gemmell was retiring after over thirty years as the programme's resident scientist. Stefan was invited to do three programmes in his stead, gradually becoming part of the new team that was taking over from the original trio.

He is engagingly frank about the attractions that broadcasting holds for him. 'Let's be honest, anybody who puts themselves in front of three million listeners or however many it is, week after week, is on something of an ego trip. You have to be. No one who is shy and retiring and shuns the public eye does that. They might have another side to their character, when they need to escape, but you must want to project yourself. You must want to be heard, seen, recognised. I think I am one of those people who need to be recognised.'

So, in 1984 he retired from the Vegetable Research Station to embark on a free-lance career – writing, broadcasting and doing a little consultancy. He also runs a photographic agency and keeps up his interest in all forms of natural history.

The Buczackis have had three houses. The first was a modern house in a small close, its garden 'quite pleasant' but Stefan was too busy with his research to devote much time to developing it. Then they moved to a Victorian town house

Above, salad and herb garden; *left,* apple trees 'Stirling Castle' and 'Catshead Codlin' frame the back door.

with a small walled area which Stefan made into a very pretty garden. Still the limited spare time showed. It was while he was working on his book on garden pests and diseases, and in it both authors acknowledge their debts to their wives for caring for the gardens they neglected. So it wasn't until 1982, with two growing boys and needing a larger house, that Stefan could consider having a garden where he would have the scope to put some of his ideas into practice. They spent a long time looking for the right house, this time insisting on a good garden too. They found just what they wanted near Stratford-on-Avon.

The oldest part of the house dates from about 1630 and the plot had been gardened for over 300 years; a document from 1860 says that even then the garden was well-established with mature fruit trees. There is just over a third of an acre of land, three-quarters at the back and a quarter at the front. It's on a soil called 'wick', good, free-draining soil enriched by silt from the river Stour and though laid out professionally twenty-five years ago, it had recently been through what Stefan calls 'a period of careful and systematic neglect'. When the Buczackis first saw it, on a cold wet day in March, it was totally overgrown; they could hardly see what they were buying as they struggled through the shoulder-high nettles, grass and foxgloves. But at least the lawns had been mown and the garden did have a framework. Outside the sitting room there was a sunken terrace surrounded by stone walls – an undertaking that would be beyond the reach of most purses today, there were some very old fruit trees and plenty of twenty-five-year-old specimen trees – a Voss's laburnum, a great white 'Tai-haku' cherry, a *Cedrus atlantica glauca*, a good sorbus, two acers, *A. negundo* and *A. platanoides* 'Crimson King', various conifers and a lovely copper beech. They also found some well-established hedges of box and yew and a twenty-foot screen of thuja and Lawson cypress; a good basis, especially for a gardener who enjoys restoration, which Stefan does. He took great delight in rescuing a huge wisteria, which he found tied in a knot, growing right up the roof and down the other side: he managed to remove it from the wall, lay it on the ground, untangle it and fix it up again. There was also an overgrown and totally derelict fig tree which he fan-trained and persuaded to yield good fruit. Inevitably there was a lot of heavy work and the first eight months were spent cleaning up, containing some of the more chaotic areas with selective weedkillers, finding out what was hidden by weeds yet worth saving, beginning to plant.

As a gardener Stefan is largely self-taught and, like his predecessor Alan Gemmell, more than willing to acknowledge how much he learns from some of his colleagues on *Gardeners' Question Time.* He had first become interested in gardening as a child, catching the enthusiasm from his father, a Polish engineer who came to England with the Polish Air Force at the beginning of the war. For the whole family the great gardening event of the year was the village British Legion Horticultural Show, where Stefan's uncle would exhibit his prize roses and his father would produce vast dahlias from the serried ranks which, even then, were not to Stefan's taste. Stefan used to enter the children's classes and his great achievement, of which he is still proud, was on one momentous occasion to grow better onions than his father. Competitiveness can begin early.

137

Rhododendron yakushimanum.

Never having been formally trained in horticulture, there is a sense in which Stefan feels that he is an amateur gardener. However, the special skills and needs that he brings to his garden put him in a different class to most amateurs. He shares with many of his colleagues the admirable conviction that if he is talking and writing about gardening all over the country, then he must grow as wide a variety as possible in his own garden so that his advice is backed, not just by academic knowledge, but by pragmatic experience. To this end he uses his space for variety rather than massing plants, a type of gardening which in any case suits his temperament – he packs his life as full as he packs his garden. His tendency to grow a little of everything in order to learn soon became confusing, so he has had to draw the line at plants he doesn't actually like. It's hard to see, however, that this makes much difference, as at the moment the list of dislikes only consists of mimulus, oenothera or evening primrose and, right at the top of the list, calceolaria.

So by the time Stefan has developed his garden the way he wants it, it will be a small living encyclopaedia of the English garden. Already there is a herb garden, a pool and a salad garden with lettuces, radishes, spring onions, tomatoes and cucumbers. The fruit cage keeps the family well supplied. It overflows with gooseberries, red, white and black currants, loganberries, tayberries, wineberries, blackberries and raspberries – early, midsummer and autumn. He's growing the gooseberries and the red and white currants on cordons, partly to save space, partly to give him practice because he hasn't done it before. There are trees, alpines, shrub roses, herbaceous borders, bulbs by the thousand, a wild garden and a cottage garden with aquilegias, forget-me-nots, buttercups and some lingering dandelions and cleavers, which his young sons are given 10p a boxful to pull up. His soil is not acid enough for azaleas and rhododendrons, so he has made a peat bed for a few choice lime-hating plants like *Rhododendron yakushimanum*.

As yet there is no greenhouse – choosing a greenhouse is something over which Stefan is going to take his time as he has strong views on the subject. He insists on a structure in sympathy both with the garden and with the house. For this situation he wants white painted wood with a brick base, putting aesthetic considerations first, despite the more laborious upkeep such a greenhouse will involve. However, the cold frame is sufficient for the pelargoniums, salad vegetables and annuals that he grows from seed. It also houses the new varieties sent by the seed companies, which are conscientiously grown before being recommended.

Stefan is not worried by fears of overplanting and has some comforting advice for gardeners who are. After he had gained his degree in botany he went to Oxford to do his D.Phil in forestry, specialising in forest diseases, and this training, when he had always to think in terms of a thirty-year rotation, has led him to feel that gardeners should be more ruthless about taking things out. With that attitude, they need not endure the gaps that are so hard to fill when planting is always carried out with the eventual size of the plant in mind.

There is one popular form of gardening conspicuous by its absence – large scale vegetable gardening. He feels he has seen enough brassicas to last him a very long while. Nor – need one say? – is he intending deliberately to produce diseases.

Stefan regards gardening as applied botany, the study of plants for their own sake. He is not one of those unfortunate botanists who spend their working lives in herbaria, never seeing a living plant. For him the interest is in the living organism, whether it is growing in a garden, in woodland, in a field or a tropical forest. He wants diversity in his garden, but it is the diversity of the botanist, not the plantsman. His distinction is precise, if personal. 'Where the plantsman is more intimately concerned with what cultivation has done to a particular species, how it has changed, how it can be used, the botanist is more interested in the natural species, unaltered by cultivation and he wants to know about representatives of several species of the genus.' He goes on to explain that while the plantsman might aspire to intimate knowledge of dozens of varieties of, for instance, the species *Chamaecyparis lawsoniana* – their colour, shape, size, habit, idiosyncracies, the botanist would prefer to study the genus in its species forms – *lawsoniana, obtusa, pisifera, henryae, thyoides, formosensis, nootkatensis*. He feels that he himself comes somewhere in between these two positions. As a botanist he is interested primarily in the species, the natural creation, but as a gardener he uses the cultivars, though he doesn't claim the range of knowledge about them that a real plantsman would have. So he collects species tulips with the ardour of the enthusiast. At present he has about twenty, ranging from the very early *turkestanica* to *sprengeri*, flowering in the early summer; while using the cultivated varieties – the lily-flowered tulips, the Darwins, the peony-flowered – as and when it suits him. He grows shrub roses, lengthening their short flowering period by choosing varieties that flower in succession and repeat flowering varieties like 'Madame Isaac Pereire' and 'Roseraie de l'Hay'; he is especially fond of some species or near-species climbers, like *R. longicuspis*, with its banana-scented flowers, *R. filipes*, 'La Mortola' and 'Mermaid' that have scarcely been changed by cultivation. Of the dahlias he chooses plants like 'Bishop of Llandaff', which is one of those closest to the wild forms. It has changed a little, but not, as Stefan says, 'into some grotesque monstrosity'.

Stefan has a great love of trees and had he been able to find a career in forestry after Oxford he would have done. So he was delighted to inherit so many mature trees, not only the framework in the main garden at the back and the fruit trees – a Victoria plum, a 'Bramley', an 'Ellison's Orange', a very old, very early cooker, 'Stirling Castle', and an even older apple tree from Gloucestershire, a 'Cat's Head Codlin', rarely seen today – but a magnificent *Magnolia soulangiana* 'Alba' and a *Prunus subhirtella* 'Autumnalis' which stand in front of the house. He was able to plant many trees that he had wanted for a long time, like *Amelanchier lamarckii*, *Magnolia grandiflora*, *Stewartia pseudocamellia*, a tree with attractive flaking bark, *Eucryphia nymansensis*, a summer-flowering evergreen tree from South America and a *Betula jacquemontii*, whose smooth bark is the purest white of all the birches.

Stefan's scientific training and background show in his approach to gardening. He accepts that there are as many ways of doing things as there are gardeners, but insists on doing them correctly – no guessing, no impulsive improvisation. If he is planting, he will plant to exactly the correct depth, at precisely the right time of year. He will use the correct fertiliser. If he has problems with pests or diseases he will use the appropriate control measures. If he is doing something for the first time, he will consult books, or talk to people who know more than he, to be sure that he finds out the best possible method. All these things give him deep pleasure.

His garden also reflects a methodical and meticulous personality, someone who always knows where he put his pencil down, who orders his time so efficiently that he will never make an unnecessary journey – if he walks from one end of the house to the other he will remember to take anything that needs to be moved. After only two years, though his meticulousness could hardly be mirrored in the whole garden, there are areas that indicate what it is to become. He is proud of the salad garden, already as neat as a text book on garden design.

As the garden reveals Stefan the scientist, so it also reveals the creative man who enjoys communication. He is at present writing a book with the working title *A Gardener's Ecology* in which he is considering the garden as a natural environment and how plants and wild life interact in it. Though this will include the whole range of gardens, from the natural to the most artificial, there is no doubt where his own garden is on the spectrum. He considers himself an ecological gardener, sympathetic to nature, never wanting to stray too far from her ways. So formal bedding is not for him, any more than were his father's serried ranks of dahlias. Indeed the only formal part of his garden at present is the

Two of Stefan Buczacki's collection of species tulips, *left, T. urumiensis,* and *right T. turkestanica.*

inherited sunken terrace and he has no wish to develop any more in that way. He is happier with the trees at the bottom of the garden, where he will leave the cow parsley and bluebells and encourage wild flowers. 'I would like to think that you could photograph at least parts of the garden so that, if you didn't know enough about the species to know that they had been collected from all over the world, it would look like a small area of natural woodland.'

So what gives Stefan his deepest pleasure in the garden? The variety? The chance to study plants at close quarters? The pleasure of doing things the right way so that the plants flourish, untroubled by pest or disease? His wife once asked him what he thought about when he was gardening; he said he thought about what it would look like in four or five years' time. What really pleases him is to see if the effect he achieves is what he had in mind when he planted. For example, while the house was still filled with decorators, he was down at the bottom of the garden, planting by the yew hedge. There is a little seat there, on one side of which he has planted a *Cytisus kewensis*, on the other a *Rosa primula*. These he hopes are going to complement each other, the yellow rose enhancing the paler yellow of the cytisus. 'Now it would give me great pleasure if one day I could sit on that seat and know that in autumn 1983, I chose those plants and created the effect that I intended.'

CLAY JONES

SEEDS OF HOPE

AFTER a lifetime of gardening, Clay Jones still cannot go into a garden centre without buying a packet of seeds – he is drawn to seeds as a bee to honey, intoxicated by the mystery they contain, the promise they hold.

It all started one spring day nearly sixty years ago. He was walking down a lane in Wales, on his way home from Sunday school, when with the imperiousness of a three-year-old, he demanded that a daisy plant should be dug out from the bank. His mother, who remained a keen gardener into her nineties, brought it home, roots and all, planted it in a jar that had contained Shippam's Paste and put it on the kitchen window sill. A few days later the small boy was beside himself with joy to find a daisy in flower. Clay Jones was hooked on gardening.

Soon a patch of the Jones's town garden in Cardigan was allocated to him for his own seeds, he was given a little wheelbarrow and even had a share in the yearly load of manure. When he was nine his territory expanded as the family moved to a twelve-acre smallholding in the country. Here they had two gardens, one an orchard where they also grew vegetables, the other a cottage garden, with flowers and soft fruit growing together. As Clay's father was away at sea much of the time, the work fell to the rest of the family and Clay loved every minute of it. So when he had to choose between science and art (a decision that in those days had to be made at about the age of thirteen), he had no difficulty in deciding on science and choosing botany and zoology. At eighteen he tried for a place at University College, Aberystwyth, but it was 1942 and the day after he heard he had been successful he received his call-up papers; his studies had to wait until the war was over.

Clay Jones is intensely Welsh – he didn't start speaking English until he was five years old, he had rarely been away from home before and was already

The porch in early days, enlivened with pot plants, while the climbers get established.

courting his wife. He was indignant at having to leave West Wales and serve in the Duke of Cornwall's Light Infantry in Bodmin. He felt cut off from his roots, remote and strange, admitting that the first six weeks in the Primary Training Corps were the most miserable of his life. After he was commissioned he was sent to Burma, which made some sense to him as at least he was in a Welsh regiment, but the moment he was demobbed he returned thankfully to Wales to take up his place at Aberystwyth.

When he had gained his degree in botany and economics he did two years post-graduate work, one at the University Botanical Garden and one in private service as a single-handed gardener. Then, equipped with both practical and theoretical experience, he began looking for permanent work. His good sense in following his instincts combined with luck and he joined a seed company, Bees of Liverpool, as a trainee, where he was assistant to one of the directors. His main responsibility was controlling production and formulating package requirements – he might need anything from 1,000 packets of a slow seller to 200,000 of a particularly popular variety. After four years he moved to Dobies, the mail order seed company and a subsidiary of Cuthbert's. He had chosen well. Clay Jones and Dobies were to stay together for twenty years and by the time he left he was a director, responsible among other things for testing seeds in their own trial grounds and compiling the catalogues.

He had found a job that satisfied him at many levels. Trained as a scientist, he understands better than most the physical conditions – moisture, temperature, depth of planting, soil type, aeration – that trigger off seed growth, but he also has a deep respect for the mystery they contain, for the way these tiny, apparently inanimate specks become beautiful flowers, vegetables, weeds. 'These little things are really miniature miracles. They are new life, it's incredible. Without seeds there is no life – the whole of life, animal, vegetable and human, depends on the germination of seeds.'

This attitude, which embraces a belief that the wonders of nature cannot be accidental, that there must be an omnipotent power which controls the universe, enabled him to pass on this enthusiasm to the girls in the seed industry who sit in front of machines, feeding in as many as 20,000 packets and millions of seeds every day in a routine, mechanical operation. Clay used to remind them that if they were ever bored they should remember their work would lead to someone else's excitement in the weeks ahead. He sometimes passed on to them a remark once made to him, 'We don't sell seeds, we sell hope.'

His awareness of the mysteries of plant growth, the magic of life, also infuses his own gardening with an excitement undimmed by repetition, as keen now as on the day when he saw a daisy bloom in a glass jar. He will sow seed with the confidence of a professional, certain that the seeds are viable and that if nature is kind and he provides the right conditions they will surely grow but, endearingly, he finds it hard to control his impatience. Knowing his lettuce seed is not going to germinate for at least a week does not stop him peering hopefully at the ground two days after sowing, eager to see the green shoots emerging from the brown soil.

Clay Jones grows several varieties of onion, both from seed and from sets. Here he is harvesting 'Kelsae'.

Summer
profusion.

The vegetable garden.

Clay's media career was launched when a former neighbour, charged with producing the first radio gardening programme in Welsh, rang him, saying with more honesty than tact, 'You're the only bloke I can think of who can speak Welsh and who knows something about gardening.' Clay was slightly nonplussed but willing to try, so in June 1960 he went to Bangor to do his first radio programme, *Garddio: Gwaith Tymorol* – a seasonal talk on sowing biennials and lawn care. This was such a success that he was given the peak time spot every Friday evening; after a few years when the programme became a panel on the lines of *Gardeners' Question Time*, it was Clay who was invited to chair it.

The countless viewers who warm to Clay's broadcasting, his wit and charm and that deep brown voice enthusing over the taste of a tomato, the texture of a potato, might think that once heard on the air he would have been instantly snapped up by every gardening programme in the country. Strangely, it was not so. 'I didn't arrive with a thunderclap,' he says happily, 'I oozed in.' This slow infusion, by way of such programmes as Percy Thrower's *Gardening Club* and Roy Hay's *In Your Garden*, led in 1976 to his becoming a member of the *Gardeners' Question Time* team. Television followed and soon Clay found himself so busy with broadcasting that he decided to go freelance. He has kept a consultancy position with Cuthbert's, acts as gardening adviser to Woolworth's, does a little voice–over advertising and answers questions at garden clinics. He has a ready pen, at the moment contributing a regular column to *Practical Gardening* and *The Lady*, he also travels the country as a judge of gardens, an experience which has led him to the conclusion that though the finest garden in Britain is Lord Aberconway's at Bodnant, though Scotland has produced more and better professional gardeners than any other country in Britain, the best

The Himalayan cowslip, *Primula florindae*, the tall yellow *P. helodoxa* and several candelabra primulas thrive at the bottom of the old quarry.

gardens are undoubtedly the English. The only fly in the ointment of his success is that honouring all his commitments does not leave him as much time as he would like in his own garden.

For twenty years Clay gardened on six inches of soil on a mountainside in North Wales. He had discovered how much can be grown by feeding generously, even when deep digging is virtually impossible, but in 1980 he decided it was time for 'a bit of horticultural paradise – a mild climate, a sheltered position, a south-facing aspect, good soil and no frost pockets'. There was another reason to move – the Joneses had become something of a tourist attraction. They used to draw the curtains in the morning to find complete strangers in their garden; on one occasion they were barely out of bed when a passer-by rang the door bell to ask Clay's advice on a sickly potato plant. It was too much. Clay has a good deal of the actor in him and enjoys being on stage (he has a superb baritone voice and might have joined the D'Oyly Carte Opera, had his mother not forbidden it), but when the curtain is down he wants to be left in peace. So they started the search, Glenys for a house, Clay, never without a spade to test the soil, more concerned to find the garden of his dreams. They found it outside Chepstow, on a quiet hillside overlooking the Severn Estuary. The cottage needed a new roof, there was no garden, unless an old hedge, a massive mock orange and a large cedarwood greenhouse can be said to constitute a garden, but there was an acre of land, a sheltered position and good soil.

There was plenty of work to be done, but that suited Clay well. He loves physical work and welcomes the exercise after hours sitting in the car (he clocks up about 30,000 miles a year with all his broadcasting and lecturing). He is one of those fortunate people who enjoy *everything* in the garden, from the first clearing of brambles, tyres and old tin cans to the final moment when he sinks his teeth delightedly into his own produce. He also enjoys construction, and has a limitless supply of sandstone from an old quarry on his land; he has already built several dry stone walls and paths and is thinking about a pool.

The Joneses prefer not so much to plan their garden as to let it grow round

Variegated leaves add distinction to a rich buddleia, *B. davidii* 'Harlequin'.

them. Clay feels that Glenys has the better eye for design, so while he tends to choose and buy plants, she places them. It was she, for instance, who decided on the two laburnum trees which grow one each side of the front gate.

Clay is clear about his priorities in the garden. He wants to be surrounded by beauty, he would never be without his fresh fruit, his vegetables or his greenhouse. Beauty in a garden can take many forms and Clay, not too fussy where it comes from, adapts willingly to his conditions. His land is surrounded on three sides by high ground and trees, well suited to the informal gardening he prefers; the soil is chalk, but he doesn't waste his energy lamenting the acid-loving plants he is denied. 'There are lots of things that grow famously on chalk – clematis, potentillas, laburnum, some acers, hebes, berberis, fruit does very well on chalk – why overload yourself?'

There are pockets of pleasure all over the garden. The walls of the house are

One of a mixture of F1 geranium hybrids, 'Sundance'.

garlanded with climbers in the style of the proverbial cottage garden. Round the porch are two roses, a 'Golden Showers' and 'Zéphirine Drouhin', his favourite climber. This lovely rose is not, however, too happy on a north wall, so it plays host to a *Clematis* 'Lasusrtern' which wanders through and thickens the lower branches. The east-facing side of the house is clothed with two more clematis, *C. montana* 'Elizabeth' and 'Nelly Moser', while passers-by will soon be able to enjoy a variegated ivy, *Hedera helix* 'Silver Queen' and a Virginia creeper, *Parthenocissus henryana*, recently planted on the west side of the house next to the road.

Round the front door, at the feet of the climbers, Clay has planted a variety of traditional cottage-garden plants and opposite the kitchen window is a border, built recently over an old cess pit, providing a home for the annuals – asters, petunias, nemesias and phlox – which Clay raises in the greenhouse. This border was continually being disturbed by the attentions of the Jones's six cats, so Glenys had the ingenious idea of placing stones among the plants to discourage them. It seems to be working. Nearby is one of the prettiest corners in the garden, which shows just what can be done with an apparently inauspicious site, tucked away at the bottom of the old quarry. It is very damp, with almost no sun, but provides text-book conditions for many of the primula family. Clay was given several packets of seed and already the Himalayan cowslip *P. florindae*, the tall yellow *P. helodoxa* and several members of the candelabra tribe are

The purple leaves of the smoke tree, *Cotinus coggygria*, contrasting with *Cornus alba elegantissima*.

established. Mixed with some astilbes and a variegated comfrey, set off by the shadowy stone, they lighten a dark area in a charming and very natural way.

This is a garden where the cultivated and the natural blend harmoniously together, an effect which owes a good deal to the banks enfolding the house and Clay's wisdom in leaving much of it as a wild garden. At the top there are primroses, cowslips, oxlips, columbines, foxgloves, violets and bluebells coming through the grass. There will soon be pockets of planting among the stones on the banks – the greenhouse is already full of ground-cover plants such as hypericum, vinca, saponaria, campanula and some lime-tolerant winter-flowering heathers. And everywhere there are ornamental trees and flowering shrubs, often bought on impulse. There are Clay's especial favourites – the shrub rose 'Nevada,' the flowering cherry, *Prunus sargentii*, the spectacular flowering almond, *Prunus tenella* 'Fire Hill' and the maple, *Acer pseudoplatanus* 'Brilliantissimum'; he is fond of variegated leaves and has put in variegated forms of buddleia, *B. davidii* 'Harlequin' and weigela, *W. florida* 'Variegata', the best of the genus, he feels. He was given a *Viburnum plicatum* 'Mariesii' on a visit to Abbotsbury Gardens; there is a witch hazel, a beech, apparently growing out of solid rock and a *Robinia pseudoacacia* 'Frisia', whose delicate golden-yellow leaves keep memories of spring alive all through the summer into autumn.

Though the trees, shrubs and flowers are transforming the face of his garden and he delights in them, television viewers who watch Clay's pleasure in harvesting onions the size of tennis balls, handling a freshly cut lettuce, sampling a crisp young carrot, will realise that his deepest satisfaction lies in the vegetable garden.

Vegetable gardening appeals to Clay on many levels. It is profitable – the Joneses only visit the greengrocer for the occasional bag of potatoes. Once the initial cost of land and tools has been met, it is cheap, especially for the gardener who makes his own compost. It provides healthy exercise. Further, the gardener himself decides on which pesticides, if any, are to be used. Clay prefers to feed the soil organically, so generously that the plants are strong and resistant to disease and he only has to use pesticides as a last resort. Finally the gardener who grows his own vegetables can choose his favourite varieties.

So the first big job Clay tackled was to hire a rotavator and prepare the large flat area, about a fifth of an acre, on the far side of the house, as a vegetable garden. Then he laid paving stones, decorated the path leading to the greenhouse with flowers, bought a frame and some cloches and began choosing his seeds.

He aims to find the variety that yields the heaviest crop while possessing the finest flavour and is continually experimenting with the new seeds that come on the market. He frequently sows several varieties of onion, both from seed and from sets, waiting to see which turn out the best; he is enthusiastic about two new broad beans, 'Jubilee Hysor' from Dobies and 'Hylon' from Sutton's; his present variety of cauliflower, 'Dok', is also fairly new – he feels it is quite the best available. He is game for anything, one year trying some runner beans given to him by someone who assured him that the pods would be two feet long and the leaves would be the size of elephants' ears. They were.

On the other hand, though he enjoys the new snap pea, which is eaten whole, he is faithful to 'Kelvedon Wonder' for an early variety and he seldom experiments with lettuce, finding that nothing beats 'Fortune'. He grows carrots, both early and main-crop, early potatoes and just a few main-crop, sweet corn, a vast range of brassicas including swedes and turnips and so many leeks that his wife can never use them all. He has discovered that it is not worth growing cucumbers in the greenhouse since he grew the outdoor variety, 'Burpee Hybrid', and harvested thirty-four cucumbers from a single plant, finding the flavour as good as anything he had grown under glass.

The magnificent cedarwood greenhouse, eighteen feet by ten, was one of the features which originally attracted him to the house. It had been put up by the parents of a previous owner, in a vain attempt to encourage him to tackle the garden, and when Clay moved in it was full of broken glass and junk. Now it plays a crucial role in his passion for growing from seed, and houses most of his tomatoes, a vegetable much associated with Clay Jones and on which he has written a book.

With his contacts in the seed industry, Clay is in an excellent position to try seeds straight from the trial grounds, before they are generally available, so he is one of the first able to pronounce on a new variety of tomato only just in the catalogues, an FI hybrid variety, 'Adonia'. It's a new Dobies introduction, the earliest they have yet produced. With only enough heat to keep off a heavy frost, Clay was harvesting them by the end of June, delighted to find they produced a good crop and had an excellent flavour. In the same year he grew five other varieties – 'Grenadier', 'Estrella', the striped 'Tigerella', 'Britain's Breakfast', a new relative of 'Gardener's Delight', and 'Moneymaker', which he is giving another chance, because he has condemned it so often in the past. His verdict: 'I reckon "Grenadier" beats the lot.'

He has recently developed his own method of growing greenhouse tomatoes. Rather than change the soil every year, he grows his plants in whalehide rings, moving them eighteen inches each year. He feeds straight into the ring, so there is no waste and the plant has the benefit of all the nourishment, while the roots go through into the soil, which is kept well watered. This way he doesn't risk disease by growing year after year in the same patch of soil, nor does he have the trouble of preparing the beds for the orthodox ring culture system. He is still experimenting and still learning. 'For ever,' he says, 'absolutely for ever.'

Fruit comes a close second to vegetables. Clay grows melons in his cold frame, raspberries, strawberries, black currants and gooseberries in the vegetable garden and fruit trees anywhere he can find a spare corner. He was one of the first people in this country to grow the self-fertile dessert cherry, 'Stella'; it was sent to him by Ken Muir who imported it from the continent. He is also prepared to wait seven years to taste 'Charles Ross', a particularly good eating apple. He has planted several other apple trees – a 'Blenheim Orange', a 'Cox's Orange Pippin', two cookers, 'Lord Derby' and 'Lane's Prince Albert'; he has a 'Victoria Plum' and three pears, 'Conference', 'Williams Bon Chrétien' and 'Doyenne du Comice', which he considers 'the pear of pears'.

The path to the greenhouse, Mr Bowles's
wallflower crowning the border.

Clay is unashamedly sentimental and sees nothing strange in talking to his
plants – they are, after all, living things. He might apologise to a flower he has
inadvertently cut down, congratulate his tomatoes on doing so well in his
absence, or reprimand an unwilling performer, sometimes with surprising
results. Once, in despair about a camellia he had tried in three different places, he
tore it out of the ground, shook it angrily and said, '*Tyfa'r diawl*', ('Grow, you
devil.') It did.

He is a great home-lover, though as oblivious in the house as he is observant in
the garden. He has been known to sleep in his newly painted bedroom without
seeing the difference. ('It's home and Glen's here, so what does it matter?') But if
Glenys so much as cuts a lettuce, or picks a branch of parsley without
permission, he will notice in an instant. But, she says, he has not yet counted the
carrots.

Clay likes nothing better than spending days in his own garden, stripped to
the waist, tending his plants. 'I like to grow plants and to grow them well. I just
get excited about everything that actually flowers.'

ROY LANCASTER

Appears regularly on BBC 2 *Gardeners' World* Specials and occasionally on *Gardeners' World*. He is currently presenting a series of seven programmes for BBC TV South, *Exploring Gardens,* and *The Great Plant Collections* for Channel 4.
He writes regularly for the Royal Horticultural Society's Journal, *The Garden,* and occasionally in *Country Life* and *The Plantsman*. Throughout the year he lectures all over the country.

PUBLICATIONS IN PRINT

Trees in Your Garden, FLORAPRINT, 1974; *Plant Hunting in Nepal*, CROOM HELM, 1981; *Trees*, MACMILLAN, 1982; (with R.H. Noailles) *Mediterranean Plants and Gardens*, FLORAPRINT, 1977; also main editorial responsibility for *Hillier's Manual of Trees and Shrubs*.

GEOFFREY SMITH

Can be heard regularly on *Gardeners' Question Time* and seen on numerous BBC Television programmes such as *Flower of the Month, World of Flowers* and *Gardeners' Direct Line*. He contributes a weekly column to *Garden News* and writes a syndicated column for *The Yorkshire Evening Post*.

PUBLICATIONS IN PRINT

Mr Smith's Vegetable Garden, BBC, 1976; *Mr Smith's Flower Garden*, BBC, 1976; *Mr Smith's Fruit Garden*, BBC, 1977; *Mr Smith Propagates Plants*, BBC, 1978; *Mr Smith's Indoor Garden*, BBC, 1979; *Shrubs and Small Trees*, HAMLYN, 1981; (with Brian Davies) *Mr Smith's Favourite Garden*, BBC, 1982; *Geoffrey Smith's World of Flowers*, BBC, Part 1 1983, Part 2 1984; *Easy Plants for Difficult Places*, HAMLYN, 1984. In preparation for 1986, *Mr Smith's Gardening Course*, BBC.

FRANCES PERRY

Presents a regular gardening programme for *Years Ahead* on Channel 4 and writes for *The Observer* and *Popular Gardening*. She was the first woman to be elected to the Council of the Royal Horticultural Society and the first woman Vice-President of the society.

PUBLICATIONS IN PRINT

Gardening in Colour, HAMLYN, 1968; *Flowers of the World*, HAMLYN, 1972; *Complete Book of House Plants and Indoor Gardening*, OCTOPUS, (hardback) 1976, (paperback) 1978; *Cacti and Succulents: Encyclopaedia of Gardening*, TIME-LIFE, 1979; (Frances Perry is also the series' European Editor); *Grown For Their Leaves*, SCOLAR PRESS, 1982; (with Roy Hay) *Tropical and Sub-Tropical Plants*, WARD LOCK, 1982; *Observer Book of Gardening*, (hardback) SIDGWICK & JACKSON, 1982, (paperback) CORONET, 1984.

BILL SOWERBUTTS

ALAN TITCHMARSH

SHEILA MACQUEEN

A founder member of Radio Four's *Gardeners' Question Time,* he still makes occasional guest appearances on the programme and contributes to regional television programmes, both BBC and ITV. He writes weekly gardening notes and supplies a query/reply service for the Catholic newspaper *The Universe* and numerous provincial newspapers from the *Liverpool Echo,* the *Oldham Chronicle* and the *Bradford Telegraph and Argus* in the north, to the *Portsmouth News,* the *West Sussex County Times* and *Kentish Times* in the south.

Can be seen twice a week on BBC's *Breakfast Time,* heard every Saturday morning on Radio Four and occasionally on Gloria Hunniford's programme on Radio 2.
He writes a weekly column in *Amateur Gardening,* is Gardening Correspondent to *Woman's Own* and a regular contributor to the Royal Horticultural Society's Journal, *The Garden.*

PUBLICATIONS IN PRINT

Climbers and Wall Plants, WARD LOCK, 1980; (with R. C. M. Wright) *Complete Book of Plant Propagation* WARD LOCK, 1981; *Allotment Gardener's Handbook,* (hardback) SEVERN HOUSE, 1982, (paperback) PENGUIN, 1984; *Guide to House Plants,* HAMLYN, 1982; *Rock Gardener's Handbook,* CROOM HELM, 1983; *How To Be a Supergardener,* WARD LOCK, 1983; *Guide to Greenhouse Gardening,* HAMLYN, 1984; *Alan Titchmarsh's Gardening Guides* (10 paperbacks) HAMLYN, 1984; *Alan Titchmarsh's Avant Gardening,* SOUVENIR, 1984;

Lectures all over the country on flower arranging, has contributed to *Gardeners' World* and Radio Four's *Woman's Hour* and writes for *Amateur Gardening* and *American Horticulture.*

PUBLICATIONS IN PRINT

Complete Flower Arranging, WARD LOCK, 1979; *Church Flower Arranging,* WARD LOCK, 1982; *More Flower Arranging From Your Garden,* WARD LOCK, 1984.

PROFESSOR
ALAN
GEMMELL

Now retired from *Gardeners' Question Time* after thirty-three years and 1,500 broadcasts, he is doing a third series of *Gemmell's Gardens.* He writes a monthly column for *The Guardian* and is Consultant Editor of *Garden Answers.* He lectures widely, prepares data-base for computer programmes on gardening and is consultant to both the City and Guilds courses for amateur gardeners and Bridgemere Nursery, possibly the largest garden centre in Europe, certainly in Britain.

PUBLICATIONS IN PRINT

Penguin Book of Basic Gardening, 1975; *Practical Gardeners' Encyclopaedia,* COLLINS, 1977.

PERCY
THROWER

Appears once a week on LBC, once a fortnight on BBC's Television programme *Blue Peter,* and occasionally on the Jimmy Young Show. He writes every week for *Amateur Gardening* and the *Daily Mail* and once a month for *Your Retirement.* In 1984 he was awarded the MBE.

PUBLICATIONS IN PRINT

Everyday Gardening in Colour, HAMLYN, 1969; *In Your Greenhouse,* HAMLYN, 1972; *In Your Garden,* HAMLYN, 1973; *Fresh Vegetables and Herbs From Your Garden,* HAMLYN, 1974; *How to Grow Fruit and Vegetables,* HAMLYN, 1977; *Encyclopaedia of Gardening,* HAMLYN, 1978; *Gardening Month by Month,* HAMLYN, 1984.

MARY
SPILLER

Takes regular gardening classes, mostly for amateurs, at Waterperry Horticultural Centre, Wheatley, Oxon, was the first regular woman presenter on *Gardeners' World* and appears occasionally on Radio Oxford.

PUBLICATIONS IN PRINT

Growing Fruit, (hardback) ALLEN LANE, 1980, (paperback) PENGUIN, 1982; *Weeds, Search and Destroy,* MACDONALD, 1985; contributor to the 1984 *Gardening Handbook,* BEACON.

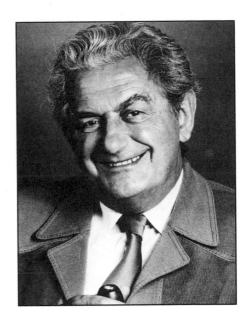

JOHN BROOKES

DR STEFAN BUCZACKI

CLAY JONES

Director and Principal of the Clock House School of Garden Design. He appears on radio and television and contributes to *Good Housekeeping, Inhabit, House and Garden, The Observer, The Financial Times, The Garden, The Sunday Times* and the American magazine *Garden Design*. He judges competitions on garden design and gives lectures and seminars in the UK, Canada, South Africa and the United States.

PUBLICATIONS IN PRINT

Room Outside, THAMES & HUDSON, 1979; *The Garden Book*, DORLING KINDERSLEY, 1984; *The Gardens of Islam*, WEIDENFELD & NICOLSON, 1985; *The Indoor Garden Book*, DORLING KINDERSLEY, 1985.

A regular member of the *Gardeners' Question Time* panel and appears on the BBC Television Programmes *Gardeners' Direct Line* and *Gardeners' World*. He writes regularly for *Amateur Gardening*, contributes to many leading magazines and newspapers and also runs a professional photographic agency.

PUBLICATIONS IN PRINT

Beat Garden Pests and Diseases, PENGUIN, 1985; *Gardeners' Questions Answered*, COLLINS, 1985; (with Keith Harris) *Collins Guide to the Pests, Diseases and Disorders of Garden Plants*, 1981, and *Collins Shorter Guide to the Pests, Diseases and Disorders of Garden Plants* 1983; (with John Wilkinson) *Gem Guide to Mushrooms and Toadstools*, COLLINS, 1982.

Co-presenter of *Gardeners' World* on BBC 2, a regular member of the panel for Radio Four's *Gardeners' Question Time* and chairs *Garddio*, the Welsh language gardening programme. He writes for *The Lady* and *Practical Gardening* and lectures extensively to Horticultural Societies and Women's Institutes.

PUBLICATIONS IN PRINT

Growing Vegetables All the Year Round, ALLEN LANE, 1978; *Growing Tomatoes, With a Note on Cucumbers, Peppers and Aubergines*, PENGUIN, 1981; *Basic Gardening*, ORBIS, 1982.

p 5 – weather vane, from a photograph by Alan Titchmarsh.

p 6 – in Bill Sowerbutts' garden, photograph by Simon Warner.

p 8 – in Sheila Macqueen's garden, photograph by Sheila Macqueen.

ROY LANCASTER

All photographs by Roy Lancaster.

GEOFFREY SMITH

All photographs by Geoffrey Smith.

FRANCES PERRY

All photographs by Frances Perry.

BILL SOWERBUTTS

All photographs by Simon Warner.

ALAN TITCHMARSH

pp 66 and 72 *(left)* by Shirley du Boulay; all other photographs by Alan Titchmarsh.

SHEILA MACQUEEN

p 81 by Shirley du Boulay; all other photographs by Sheila Macqueen.

ALAN GEMMELL

All photographs by George Young Photographers.

PERCY THROWER

All photographs by Percy Thrower.

MARY SPILLER

p 110 *(left)* and p 116 *(left and right)* by Stefan Buczacki; p 118 by Bruce Coleman Ltd.; all other photographs by Mary Spiller.

JOHN BROOKES

All photographs by John Brookes.

STEFAN BUCZACKI

All photographs by Stefan Buczacki.

CLAY JONES

p 142 by Tony Evans, courtesy of the *Sunday Express*; pp 147 and 153 by Shirley du Boulay; all other photographs by Stefan Buczacki.